Individuality and Primal Unity: Ego's Struggle for Dominance in Today's World

by Jim Willis

Volume I: Ego and Earth Magic (*Merlin the Magician: A Mystery for the Ages*)

Volume II: Ego and the Hero (*Robin Hood: Victory Through Defiance*)

Volume III: Ego and Innocence (*Little Snow-White: A Road Map for Our Time*)

Individuality and Primal Unity:
Ego's Struggle for Dominance in Today's World
Volume II: Ego and the Hero (Robin Hood: Victory Through Defiance)
© 2022 by Jim Willis
ISBN 978-1-989940-41-9
Dimensionfold Publishing

Preface

At some point in the distant past, a remote, ancient ancestor began to think in terms of the word "I." He or she became the first to understand the concept of individuality — the idea that "I" am separate and distinct from "You" and harbor different needs and desires. In that moment, *Ego* was born and humankind was metaphorically cast out of Eden. The struggle for existence, now understood in terms of a struggle for individual survival, began. No longer was identity found in species recognition. The "One" became the "Many." Unity was fractured. Henceforth the individual would reign supreme. "Look out for #1" became a human mantra and the quest for individual power began.

It continues to this day. Ego didn't necessarily lose the ability to feel empathy and compassion, but from the very beginning its primary instincts were for personal protection, survival, and growth. This has led to such concepts as the divine right of kings, class warfare, political dominance, top-heavy economic control over the means of industrial production, and monetary benefits for the few as opposed to the many.

Especially in these days of social media, every morning it has become standard procedure for many people to stare into the allegorical mirror of their computer screen, affirm their social status based on the number of responses they generated overnight, and ask, "Who is the fairest of them all?" It would appear as though Snow-White's evil stepmother has been reincarnated and lives on in modern society. Increasingly, we find ourselves living in Ego's home country, a land called Narcissism.

How do we resist such an insidious enemy? As always, those who came before left us clues to follow. Their wisdom forms the basis of this trilogy.

Those who created the old, familiar myths, legends, and bedtime tales were well aware of the dangers of Ego. They might not have understood the struggle in modern, psychological terms. But they were intuitive enough to compose stories about it. In these imaginative tales they pitted Ego against the healing magic of Earth Energy, the ancestral Eden from whence Ego had sprung.

Eventually, the civilized "Ego of the City" sought to destroy its wild and untamed predecessor who still lived out in the natural world. It is not by accident that the biblical story begins in a Genesis garden and ends in a Revelation city. It is revealing when Hebrew mythology records that right after the first murder was perpetrated because of a bruised ego, the murderer, Cain, went out and built a city east of Eden. Ever since, the metaphorical story of civilization is the story of the power struggle between cities. Industrial civilization, not the army, destroyed the American Indians. Today's headlines remind us again and again that the technology of development is a two-edged sword. Urban blight is a principal enemy of nature's resources. These stories mark the progress of Ego's conquests.

We will explore this subject by means of an in-depth analysis of three ancient tales. Each story will be developed in a separate book which can stand alone on its own, but will be part of a trilogy that encompasses the three stages of Ego's rise to dominance.

Part I: Ego and Earth Magic (*Merlin the Magician: A Mystery for the Ages*)

In the Arthurian legends, Merlin the Magician is pitted against dark energies summoned by Ego, who seeks to destroy the source of ancient Earth Magic. At the end, Ego appears to be victorious. Merlin is presented as the last of the old ones to be associated with natural magic, and is entombed in a crystal cave, deep in the bowels of the earth.

But just as in the Christ story, the Arthurian tale of the *Once and Future King*, the American Indian Tecumseh legends, and the Tolkien Ring Cycle, there is the promise of a return. Merlin will one day awake to be reunited with Arthur. The union of Earth Magic and spiritual Camelot will be spread abroad "on earth, as it is in heaven."

Until then, however, with ancient Earth Magic seemingly destroyed, or at least imprisoned, Ego is free to strike out at those humans who still follow the old, earth-based, natural ways.

Part II: Ego and the Hero (*Robin Hood: Victory Through Defiance*)

The Hero, Robin Hood, is a nature man who is at home in the wild forests of Sherwood. He defies the ego-centric, power-hungry sheriff of Nottingham, who remains ensconced in his fortified urban castle. In the end, the Hero teaches us to be victorious by defying Ego's claims on personal freedom and individual choice. Robin Hood refuses walls and the loss of independence. His final victory is assured with the return of King Richard, and his marriage to Marian reunites nature and civilization into one spiritual landscape.

Part III: Ego and Innocence (*Little Snow-White: A Road Map for Our Time*)

In the story of *Little Snow-White*, Queen Ego, secure in her castle, seeks to destroy Snow-White, who represents Intuitive Innocence. Snow-White lives in the wild forest "across the seven mountains" with the seven dwarfs. In the end, Innocence triumphs over Ego through her interaction with earth energies. As in the story of Robin Hood, once victory is assured, her marriage to the prince from a faraway, mysterious land, unites the physical and the spiritual aspects of life in our perception realm. (Spoiler alert: Awakening Snow-White with a kiss is a Disney abomination. In the original version, she awakens through interaction with Earth Energy!)

In the first tale, Earth Magic is seemingly neutralized and imprisoned in the crystal cave of the earth. This is a picture of 21st century life. Civilization has brought about a feeling of deadness when it comes to the natural world. We have separated ourselves from the very Earth Mother who gave us birth. Ego can never-the-less be defeated by energies and forces inherent in the natural world. Therein lies our hope and our salvation. Earth Energy slumbers, but is not defeated. Not yet.

In the next two stories we explore the current status of Ego in today's world. It battles both the Hero and the Innocent, but Earth Magic still comes to the aid of the deserving if we are attuned to its beckoning call.

All three stories reach their climax when hope arrives in the guise of "Royalty" from outside, a reference to spiritual help that is always available to those who are in touch with nature. In the case of Merlin, spiritual aid comes from Arthur the King. Robin Hood welcomes the return of King Richard. Snow-White is joined by the mysterious prince. None of these visitors arrives to "save the day." Rather, they make their entrance after the battle is already won. Their presence may have been subtle and understated, but their ancient magic and power was none the less available.

So it is that in our civilized world, invented and dominated by materialistic Ego, selfish individuality often appears to be victorious, while archaic Earth Magic seems imprisoned in a tomb. But in the end, spiritual energies from the natural world, which is a manifestation of the Source of All That Is, offers the hope of triumph over seemingly impossible odds.

Individualistic Ego's demise, we are assured, is certain, and the unity of Eden will again be restored when spirituality arrives in the flesh to participate in the final victory.

In the end, this is a trilogy of hope.

Robin Hood:
Victory Through Defiance

Jim Willis

Table of Contents

Introduction – page 1
Part I: The Land – page 9
    Civilization and Wildness – page 27
Part II: The Hero – page 45
    Robin Hood: The Civilized Wild Man – page 51
Part III: The Antagonists – page 59
    Prince John: The Usurper – page 67
    The Sheriff of Nottingham: The Patriarchy's Political Puppet – page 81
Part IV: The Merry Men – page 95
    Little John: Strength and Allegiance – page 101
    Much, the Miller's Son: Man of the Earth – page 115
    Will Scarlet: Male Beauty and Strength – page 121
    Alan-A-Dale: The Arts – page 133
    Friar Tuck: Rugged Spirituality – page 141
    The Saracen: A Mysterious Stranger – page 151
    Maid Marian: Female Energy Enslaved on a Pedestal – page 159
Conclusions – page 169
Further Reading – page 177

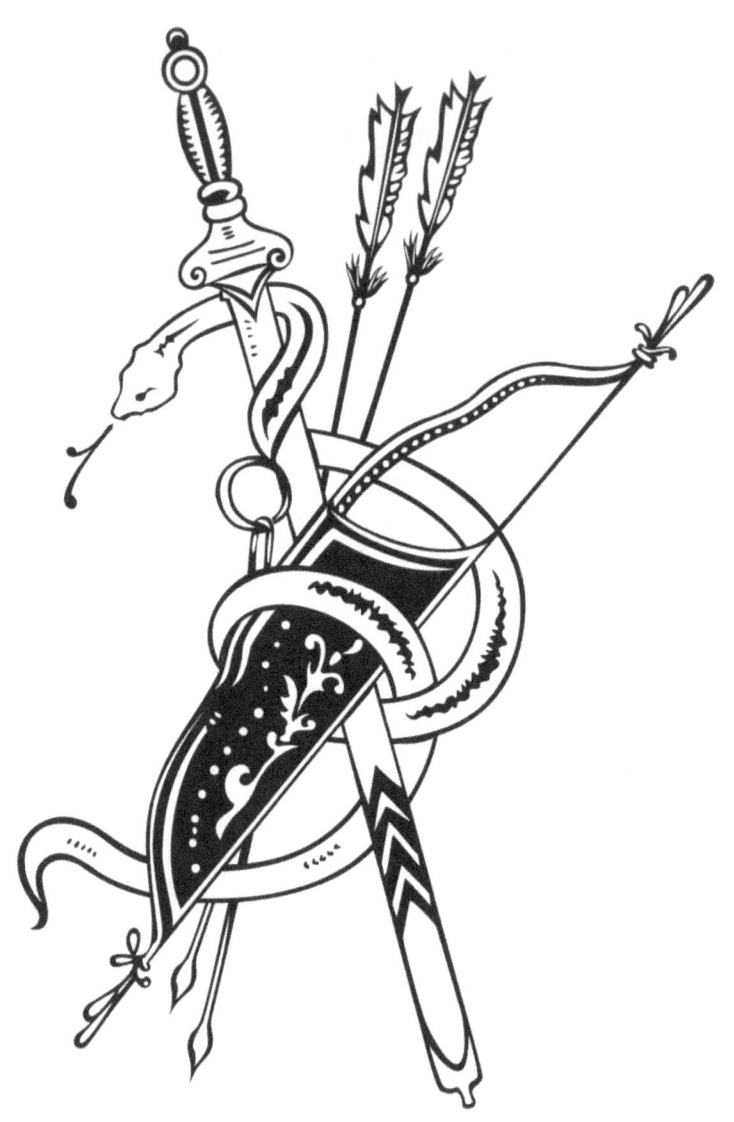

Introduction

*Lithe and listen, gentleman,
That be of freeborn blood;
I shall you tell of a good yeoman,
His name was Robin Hood.*

*Robin was a proud outlaw,
Whiles he walked on ground;
So courteous an outlaw as he was one
Was never none found.*

From **A Gest of Robyn Hode** (anonymous)

England is a haunted land. It's not that it's a place of ghosts and things that go bump in the night, although many claim that is, indeed, the case. If ghost sightings were to be plotted on a map, England would demonstrate the densest concentration of such stories anywhere in the world. But more than that, it's haunted by legends, myths, stories, and, more than anything else, history. From the Green Man to King Arthur, from Lady Godiva to Avalon, and from Merlin to the Lady of the Lake, the land fairly shimmers with exotic tales that remain among the best-known examples of mystery and magic that exist anywhere in the world. Filled with henges, barrows, monoliths, and mysterious stone circles, watched over by the "old ones," fairies, and "little people," it's a place wherein the difference between night and day is marked by much more than degrees of light and darkness. But standing above and beyond them all is the legend of Robin Hood.

He is not a creature of the night, who secretly steals down from the hollow hills to partake of roadside offerings left for the gods. No, he is a flesh-and-blood man who performs his deeds in the light of day. He is a hero of the common man, who takes from the power-hungry rich in order to give to the downtrodden poor. He is a patriot, loyal to the rightful king while defying the illegal governors who seek power for their own greedy ambitions. Such is his carefree personality and devil-may-care, flamboyant persona that he attracts to himself all manner of companions who bask in his reflected glory. Mixing supreme confidence with likable humility, he garners to himself legends and stories that only grow with the telling.

Did an historical Robin Hood of such legend and myth once exist? Of course not. If a person like that ever lived, he would certainly prove to be a disappointment. But he *should* have, so he lives today. He's bigger and more noble than ever. And we are all the better for it.

It is possible, of course, that his legend is based on a composite of actual, historical, figures. Romantic historians love to search old records for similar names and identities, people who might somehow "prove" that a historical Robin Hood once walked the fabled glades of Sherwood Forest, living a civilized life while feasting in grand style off the "king's" deer, washed down by mugs of ale. The searches usually lead to dead ends, of course. The name Sherwood Forest doesn't even appear in the sagas until four centuries after the time the legends began to circulate. In the beginning, if a real Robin Hood ever existed, he seems to be a Yorkshire man. But that's okay. Legends aren't about history. They're concerned with reality. In other words, mythology.

That leaves Robin free to be a larger-than-life man of action, extremely proficient with both blade and staff, while being one of the most superb archers who ever lived, matched only by William Tell, Legolas the Elf, Hawkeye the Avenger, and Cupid, son of the goddess Aphrodite.

Our purpose in this book is not to explore the history, real or imagined, of Robin Hood. It makes no difference if he, or someone like him, once existed. Such a historical search is fun, and maybe even a good thing. But the emphasis of this book is not on the man behind the myth. We will instead look at the myth itself. It makes no difference in our study when, where, or *if* he lived in the flesh. Our purpose is to delve into the story that has grown up around him over the years.

There is a reason why legends stand the test of time. They are repeated over and over again down through generations because they reveal as much about *us* as they do about the source of their inspiration. We identify with them. We devour the old tales because they remind us what it means to live an authentic life in *our* circumstances—in *our* lives. The story-tellers give their heroes attributes to which we aspire. When someone is brave and forthright, we are reminded that these are attitudes we want to demonstrate when difficult times assault us. When someone triumphs over adversity, it gives us hope. It's as simple, and as complicated, as that. Heroes provide a template. They show us how to act. We want to emulate them. Or, at the very least, we want to live vicariously through their exploits.

To approach the story of Robin Hood in this way is to read it in a completely different manner than we did as children. Back then, we envied the physical talents. We wanted to be able to fight, shoot a bow, wield a sword, handle a quarter staff, leap small buildings at a single bound, and triumph unequivocally over the forces of evil. We wanted a joyful ending wherein all the good guys could live happily ever after—and win the hearts of all the beautiful girls.

There's nothing wrong with any of this. It's perfectly appropriate for children to have such heroes. But, to quote the apostle Paul in 1st Corinthians 13:11: "When I was a child, I spoke as a child, I understood as a child, I thought as a child: but when I became a man, I put away childish things."

As adults, it's now time "put away" our childlike means of understanding and steep ourselves in the wisdom inherent in the stories. The old-timers crafted their tales on many levels. They spoke to a wide audience. One of the deepest and most satisfying levels of wisdom found in

Robin Hood involves understanding how to personally respond to a world in which ego reigns supreme. How do we live in a world replete with narcissism?

When our rulers govern out of a quest for power, when our bosses try to build a reputation for themselves that rests on *our* work and ability, when our friends attempt to use us to accomplish their own ends, Robin Hood offers us an example to follow. Sometimes the only way to achieve real freedom is to fight back, honorably and heroically, even if it means leaving the comfortable world that has been our home and is, indeed, our birthright. At such times, wallowing in self-pity, moaning "woe is me!", telling ourselves that life isn't fair, or that we are being treated with contempt, just won't cut it. There is a time to say, in the words of country song writer David Allen Coe, "Take this job and shove it!" There is a time to recognize that maybe the rat race needs one less rat. There is a time to stand up to friends and family, drop out of an inauthentic life, and start to live a life of freedom.

It might mean leaving the comforts of the city for work in the country. It might involve learning new skills, making new friends, and developing different means of support. But it can be done, honorably and with passionate joy. Robin Hood shows us how.

When his life was turned upside down, when, through no fault of his own, he lost his inheritance and position, when threatened with the loss of his freedom, he chose to make substantial changes, and became a better man for it.

This is what the old story-tellers sought to convey as they created their tales, surrounded their hero with a metaphorical cast of characters, placed him in unique situations, and allowed him to react. Robin Hood is more than a historical representation. He is a powerful symbol.

This is what we can glean from his story. He didn't live back *then*. He lives *now*, today, in each and every one of us. He is every man and every woman. As he battles Prince John the usurper and the narcissistic Sherriff of Nottingham, as he faces off against a corrupt church hierarchy who use religion to further their own ends, as he plunders the ill-gotten gains of the ego-encrusted rich in order to distribute them to the deserving poor, he wages a one-man war against the very religious and economic forces that make the world go around today.

In short, his story is much more than one of adventure and swashbuckling daring-do. It offers a template, a guide, to resisting ego in its many evil contemporary forms while coming out on top in the end. Above all, it shows us how to fight the good fight with fierce, unmitigated and unconquerable *joie de vivre*, a joy of life. Sometimes we all can benefit from being pushed out of our ruts—even comfortable ones. When that happens, it doesn't mean the end has come. Maybe it just marks a new beginning!

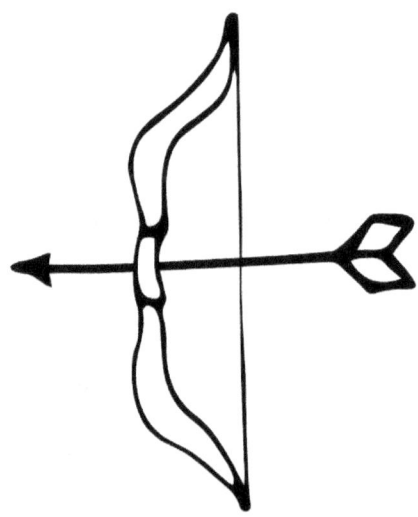

Part I: The Land

There's an archer dressed in Lincoln green,
a friend to those in need.
No thief is he who offers encouragement
to people with kind deeds.
A jealous sheriff, dressed in black,
wants to rule Ole Nottingham,
A township near Sherwood Forest,
the sheriff wants to command.

(From *Robin Wears No Hood: Not for any Contest*
Lin Lane, 2016)

If you drive north and a little west from London for about three hours, or for a bit more than 240 kilometers (150 miles) following the M1 highway, you will come to the site of Sherwood Forest. Legend, if not dry old history books, has it that this was the home of Robin Hood and his Band of Merry Men.

In the early 1200s, which is considered by many scholars to be the time Robin trod these woods, Sherwood covered more than 100,000 acres, roughly a fifth of the county known as Nottinghamshire. Evidence of flint tools used by pre-historic hunter/gatherers have been dug up, indicating the area has been popular for thousands of years. It had been a wooded forest ever since the end of the last glacial epoch, and was designated a private royal hunting ground. Any wild game was considered to be the property of the king, so when a commoner killed an animal for his family's table, he was, technically, a poacher. Eating "the king's deer" was a capital offence, punishable by severe methods, including death.

Running right through the middle of the forest lay the Great North Way, a highway of sorts, connecting London and York. Any travelers usually went heavily armed in order to protect themselves from robbers who lived outside the law. Ever since those times, such thieves have been called "outlaws."

The place was first recorded as a geographical area unto itself in 958 AD. It was called Sciryuda, which means "the woodland belonging to the shire." It became a royal hunting preserve in 1066, following the Norman invasion of England, and was a favorite hunting spot of King John and Edward the First. The ruins of John's hunting lodge still stand near the village of Kings Clipstone.

In those days, "forest" didn't simply refer to a stand of trees. It was a legal term, signifying an area subject to royal laws put in place to protect timber and wild game. A "forester" didn't just keep track of the health of trees. Sometimes called agisters, wardens (verderers) or rangers, these were all men hired by the Crown to patrol the area. They were well-armed, and were expected to employ even lethal force when necessary.

During the time of the Roman occupation, and extending back all the way to the iron age, farming communities, some of which exist to this day, cleared large areas of land, so it wasn't all covered with trees and woods in various stages of development. Farmsteads were quite common. Today, Scandinavian influences can be found in towns that end in the letters b and y, such as Thorresby. Danish names tend toward ending in "thorpe," as in Gleadthorpe. Town names ending in "feld," as in Mansfield, reveal their Roman roots.

The Sherwood Forest of Robin Hood's day would have been comprised of birch and oak trees, interspersed with large, rather open areas of sandy heath and grassland, perfect for grazing herds of deer—creatures of the edges more than dwellers in thick, virgin timber, which is not conducive to low growing shrubs and plants. This was productive, managed land which, when properly harvested, could provide a good living for a rural population. Dead trees and brush, called "underwood," was gathered and either sold or used in individual dwellings. Techniques called "coppicing" and "pollarding" produced poles and laths for building material. Oak bark was used to tan leather. Acorns were fed to domestic pigs. Cattle and sheep shared the pasture-like glades with deer.

The forest was home to more than farmsteads. By the 12th and 13th centuries, Christian monastic orders thrived on large estates provided by the Crown. Newstead, Thurgarton, and Rufford were examples of just a few of them. The market at Market Warsop is just one example. Most of these faded into history when Henry VIII invoked what is now called *The Dissolution* in 1536. Monastic land was sold into private ownership and, over the years, usually was converted into country homes and estates. But even then, a few hundred years after the time of Robin Hood, the peasant classes managed to hold on to a centuries-old way of life.

In 1604, King James I authorized a translation of the Bible that soon became the standard version still in use today. But he had other interests that went beyond biblical studies. He loved to hunt in Sherwood, but his son, Charles I, was the last to use it for that purpose. Charles was executed during the English Civil Wars, and for a long time the forest suffered from lack of management. Two hundred years later, after large areas had been sold or given to nobles and various favorites of the court, private landlords created the estates of Thoresby, Rufford, Welbeck, Wollaton, and Newstead. The aristocratic nature of these estates drew to themselves the title of "Dukeries," and became very profitable. Timber used in building, furniture production, and the insatiable need for ships to supply the British navy, provided the now-private owners with a good income.

By 1830, the last of the official "Crown's land" had been sold. To Robin Hood, all this was in the future. In his day, the forest was inhabited by outlaws, outcasts, and robbers, all hiding from the law. But according to legend, he was the greatest and most noble of them all. His story was one of freedom and justifiable thievery. If the rulers of the land took advantage of the common people, the common people felt they had the right to fight back.

Whether or not they ever did any of the things Robin was supposed to have done, no doubt such stories fired the imagination of the common folk, and gave them all hope. This was the field that produced a bountiful harvest of swashbuckling tales and legends of heroes. But in our day, the symbolism becomes just as important. Maybe even more so. Between York and London, two great centers of civilization, lay the wild land of Sherwood Forest. To travel from one place to the other, you had to pass through the wilderness.

York and London are separated by some 200 miles (279 kilometers). Before we can understand what they symbolize in the sagas of Robin Hood, we need to compile at least a little history.

The Norman Conquest of England in 1066 had a huge impact on the village of York. The Cathedral of Minster was, in effect, re-founded. Gates and battlements built during the time of the Romans were enhanced and fortified. Two Norman castles were built to control the rivers that were the life-blood of the town. Parish churches, royal mansions, houses, monasteries, and stone bridges were built. By the time of the Robin Hood stories, York was an economic powerhouse. In 1212 it obtained a royal charter, and a civic government was developed.

All this translates into money, which flowed into and out of the city. And the river of money flowed right through Sherwood Forest on its way south to London and Westminster. But wherever we find money, we find corruption, even in the church of that day. King John is usually referred to as "Prince" John in the Robin Hood tales, because he wasn't king yet. His brother, Richard, was off fighting in the Third Crusade. That didn't stop John from, for all practical purposes, usurping the crown for himself. To say he was unpopular is to put it mildly.

In March of 1201, for instance, he went to York to meet the Scottish king. The meeting never took place, but he was so disappointed in the turnout of citizens of York that he fined each and every one of them £100, "because they did not come out to meet him when he arrived at York, and that they might be quit because they did not accommodate the king's crossbowmen, and for having acquittance of the hostages which the king exacted from them at his pleasure."

He made annual visits between 1204 and 1210, ostensibly to purchase wine. York fishermen were warned to have a good supply of fish ready "against the coming of the king." By 1213, Yorkshire timber was being cut to strengthen defenses, and the "sheriff," who was to become one of Robin's most infamous foes, was mounting a garrison to keep the peace. When John launched a campaign to subdue the north and east country, he made York his headquarters.

During this time, England had no fixed capital city. It moved with the king. But the royal treasury and financial records were kept in Westminster, a small town just upriver from London. London, however, was on its way to becoming a center of trade.

In 1066, on Christmas Day, William the Conqueror had been crowned king of England at Westminster Abbey. By 1176, the first stone London Bridge had been built. Various guilds of craftsmen were established.

Threadneedle Street was where the tailor's worked. Cows were kept on Milk Street. There was a great livestock market at Smithfield. London was about to boom, even though plague was a constant threat.

To summarize all this, two big centers of economic commerce and trade were separated by Sherwood Forest. Is it any wonder that tales of outlaws and robbers began to be bandied about and set to music? It was a time of ballads, sung by troubadours, that elevated heroes who fought on the side of the common man against the economic power of the elites who sought riches from the subjects they believed owed them allegiance.

What this means is that England of the early 13th century became, through song and story, a rich ground for symbolism in the eternal struggle between the power-hungry desires of the rich who sought to subjugate the poor. The centers of ego-boosted urban economic commerce were pitted against the freedom of the natural world, free of class and caste. The people who shaped the symbolism, and presented it in metaphor, were the bards, who wrote and sang the songs. As always, the artists were those who led the way in giving voice to the population in general. They spoke for the common folk, and their ballads live on to this day.

What was the story they told? Just this.

Sherwood Forest came to represent the wild lands that gave us birth and nurtured us for millennia after millennia. But we, as a species, grew away from Mother Earth. We gravitated out from our life-supporting center, the womb of our existence. We began to seek after power and economic gain, symbolized by the two opposite poles of London and York. It's no accident that, according to the Bible, the first "outlaw," Cain, who murdered his brother, immediately went out and built a city. Cities are built on commerce. Commerce is easily perverted into avenues of personal greed. People naturally engage in commerce in order to make money. But, again according to the Bible, "the love of money is the root of all evil." Making money is, obviously, a profitable occupation. But when is enough, enough? Far too often, when someone makes a lot of money, they want to make more. The temptation is to continue on after we make a fortune, not stop.

Ego is at the root of it all. Money is usually earned by hiring underlings to work for us. They are the ones who produce the profit. Rich people couldn't get rich without, in one way or another, exploiting poorer people. CEOs make hundreds, sometimes thousands, of times more than the people who keep their companies manufacturing whatever it is they provide. For every person who becomes rich, there are thousands more who scrape by on a barely livable yearly salary. Communism, Socialism, Capitalism, and every other historical, economic "ism" that has been invented to control the flow of wealth, recognized this inherent flaw in human nature. It has been going on ever since human beings first invented civilization. And as people become wealthy, it is all too easy for them to begin to think they are somehow better, and more privileged, than everyone else.

But for purposes of the Robin Hood saga, let's look not so much at the economic realities as the ego-centered people behind them—the ones who profited off the labor of others, often by threat of violence. At the heart of it all lay the pathological narcissism of those in power who wanted even more power. Rich people who wanted more money. Comfortable people who wanted more comforts. Ego-centered rulers who wouldn't stop until they lived the lives of gods on earth.

Voltaire once said: "The best government is a benevolent tyranny tempered by an occasional assassination."

He was right. Benevolent monarchies work about as well as any form of government. That's why Christians and Jews await the coming of the Messiah, who will institute a benevolent theocracy on earth. But throughout history, such governments have been few and far between, and they never last very long. For every "good king Richard," there is an evil prince John, waiting in the wings.

Between York and London, however, the two symbolic centers of greed and power, there lay the mysteries of the wildland—Sherwood Forest. Once you ventured outside the shell of civilization, you entered tera incognita. Or perhaps we should say "re-entered," because this, you will remember, is the natural world, the world that gave us birth, the world we left to build our cities and establish our forms of government and commerce.

It's a world where values are completely different. For the most part, a dollar bill is worthless in the wild, unless you need some paper to start a fire. You need a different set of skills out there, and a different philosophy towards life. You need to be tough and resourceful. You need to depend on your own ability to survive. Many a captain of industry wouldn't last more than a few days on his own in real wilderness, without help from those who provide his pampered existence in the soft confines of his comfortable home.

Out there in the wild is where humans developed for thousands upon thousands of years. There is where we became a people. Civilization, remember, is only about twelve thousand years old, if that. For at least two hundred thousand years before the first city was built, the wilderness was our home. If anything, the wild is reality. Cities are a temporary aberration.

But when we left the wild, when we moved indoors and built walls around ourselves, we quickly forgot how to live in reality. The wild became a fearful place. It was no longer our home, our womb, our place of nurture. In the city, meat comes wrapped in cellophane packages. Milk comes in cartons; vegetables in cans. No longer do we feel at home in the environment that gave us birth. It is foreign to us; a fearful place.

But one's man fears are another man's freedom. Robin Hood became popular because he left the comforts of civilization. He was shoved out into the wild, where most men would have soon shriveled up and died. Instead, he thrived on it, all the while demonstrating a confidence that at times bordered on arrogance. When the law became a perverted force of power employed by the rich and powerful, he moved outside the system. He became an "out-law." He took the cards he was dealt, and played them with style and grace. Where others would have perished, he became a hero.

In short, he trumped the cultural system built by ego-centered, power-hungry narcissists, and lived life on his own terms. He made up his own rules, and they had to do with remaining loyal to the rightful king, rewarding friendships and honorable behavior, and championing those who needed his help.

Perhaps that's the first and best lesson we can take from the Robin Hood sagas. They teach us how to live when, usually quite by accident, we discover that we, too, have ventured out of our own reality. At such times we find ourselves siphoned off, working our lives away at dead-end jobs, in order to squeeze by while those above us on the social scale profit from our labor. We wonder how it happened. Who created a world where everything we do depends on our having a job and a boss, whether we like it or not? Without employment, we have no way of providing for our own health. We have no way of buying a home or a car. We can't provide food for our family's table.

It wasn't always like that. Way back, when our species was much younger, people knew how to provide for themselves. That is no longer the case. And as much as we might want to drop out and go it alone, economic and social forces have made it almost impossible to do so.

How many of us have daydreamed about moving to a desert island, or venturing forth into the wilderness to live off the land? How often have we read about Robinson Crusoe, the Swift Family Robinson, Jeremiah Johnson, Daniel Boone, or one of the many stories that have grown up about people who decided they had enough, and sailed, trekked, or simply wondered off into the wild?

The wild has become a fearful place to most of us. We walk up to the edge, stare into the unknown, and then, too often, meekly turn away and retreat back to our hemmed-in existence. The romance of Robin Hood is that he took the extra step. He remains an inspiration for everyone who would like to do what he did, and do it with his style.

Whether or not he ever actually ever achieved the adventures credited to him really doesn't matter. What's important is the essence of the story. But remember that in order to achieve what he did, we have to dare our own symbolic Sherwood Forest—the place that lies at the center of the two opposite metaphorical poles of York and London. There comes a time when we need to learn new skills, new ways of approaching life, new methods of operation, new ways of thinking. And the place to learn all that is the place that originally gave us birth. It's a wild place, full of fearsome beasts, untamed people, and mysteries. But, as we shall soon see, there were many who dared to do just that—to join Robin out in the wild, learn from him, and live in freedom.

It was no accident that history refers to these brave lads as "merry," not sad and defeated. They were Robin's "Band of Merry Men."

Where is your Sherwood Forest? What do you need to learn in order to live there? How much courage do you have, especially on those long dark nights when you lay awake, contemplating what has become of your life? At such times you need to remember that out there in the wilderness, free from the ego-centered rules of those who would hem you in, there still lies a wild land of mystery. It is different for each of us. But it is there. And it beckons us forward.

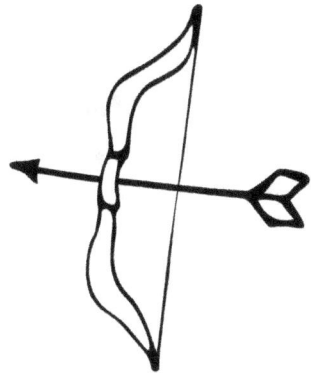

Civilization and Wildness

Something there is that doesn't love a wall,
That wants it down.

(From *Mending Wall*, by Robert Frost)

It probably is entirely possible to build a strong sense of spirituality while surrounded by a city. But it is highly unlikely.

Such a statement needs some explanation, because I'm sure that many people, especially those who live in cities, have already begun to howl in anger and wrath. But hear me out. It's important.

First a caveat. For those who know my history, yes, I live in the woods. Days go by when I don't see or hear anyone. You have every right to consider me prejudiced. But I have plenty of city experience. I didn't move out here until I was 62 years old, and I did it deliberately, for the very purpose of testing my theory. Perhaps Thoreau said it best:

I went to the woods because I wished to live deliberately, to front only the essential facts of life, and see if I could not learn what it had to teach, and not, when I came to die, discover that I had not lived. I did not wish to live what was not life, living is so dear; nor did I wish to practice resignation, unless it was quite necessary. I wanted to live deep and suck out all the marrow of life, to live so sturdily and Spartan-like as to put to rout all that was not life, to cut a broad swath and shave close, to drive life into a corner, and reduce it to its lowest terms ...

I am also, I readily admit, prejudiced in other ways. I have had this argument with many people, and I have had the privilege of knowing quite a few who thought they were living a deeply spiritual life. They practiced yoga every day, indulged in a daily regimen of meditation, and read all the right books. Quite a few even posted pictures of fairies and elves on their Facebook page. But I have yet to discover even one who had the kind of spiritual life that I consider deep and rich. Certainly, none who I want to emulate. Of course, I don't either, but I really try.

Consider the examples of some spiritual masters of the past:

- Moses purportedly spent 40 years in the wilderness before he had his experience at the burning bush. He had to leave the fleshpots of Egypt behind before he was ready to move forward. And ever after, for the rest of his life, when he needed to confront YHVH, Jehovah, he went alone up to the top of a mountain.
- Jesus spent 40 days in the wilderness before he was ready to confront the devil. And ever after, he felt the need to get away from his disciples from time to time, in order to spend a few hours alone with God.
- Mohammad went alone to his famous wilderness cave where he communed with the messenger of Allah who gave him the *Koran,* and accompanied him on his various journeys of the spirit.
- Siddhartha had to leave behind his plush life in the palace and journey alone for many years before he was ready to obtain the spiritual insight that made him the Buddha.

- Native Americans who practiced the discipline of the Vision Quest knew they had to go alone into the wild in order to meet their totem animal/spirit guide.

The old spiritual had it right. "You have to walk this lonesome valley by yourself."

This is not to say we all have the means or opportunity to follow the path of solitude. Nowadays, most of us don't. That's simply a fact of life in the "civilized" world of the 21st century. But the truth remains that our modern lifestyle, shaped by a culture we artificially created, makes it almost impossible to obtain a deeply spiritual life by following the old, tried-and-true methods.

Look at it this way, if you are still in doubt. It's simply a matter of biology. We inhabit the same bodies that the ancient spiritual giants, the Founders who gave us our mythology, inhabited. In all of the important ways, we are just like them. We evolved within the confines of a five-fold wall comprised of our senses. Smell, sight, taste, touch, and hearing are how we experience the world. This sense fence filters out the majority of energies we experience. If it were otherwise, we would be overwhelmed.

But we have created an artificial barrage of energy that, minute by minute, assaults our senses. The world surrounding most of us features a cacophony of sounds, smells, and sights. Open your window, if you live in a populated area, and really listen to the noise you have trained yourself to ignore. You will be amazed. The world to which we have become accustomed is a world the old-timers never imagined.

They listened to natural bird calls and the whisper of wind in the trees. We are accosted by the sound of traffic on the nearby Interstate, to say nothing of the jacked-up rap music from the nearby boom box. They smelled pine scents and autumn leaves. We endure gas fumes and factory smoke. They moved at the speed comfortably furnished by two legs or, at most, a horse. We drive from appointment to appointment at speeds they could never have achieved.

Even indoors, with windows tightly shuttered against the outdoor world, the various sounds from refrigerators, air conditioners, and heating units hum away in the background. And where the ancients saw familiar evening stars and knew what phase the moon was in, we see only incessant LED lights informing us that our various technological devices are off. Who ever thought that one up? A light to tell us that the appliance attached to it is off? Is that really necessary?

Multi-tasking is what makes our world go 'round. We hit the ground running each morning. How can we possibly expect to slow down in only a few minutes, assuming we even attempt to sit down in order to take stock of things?

Next time you are stuck in a doctor's waiting room or waiting in a crowded airport somewhere, look around and count the number of people who are comfortable just sitting still. Almost all of them will be staring intently at hand-held screens of some kind. Few and far between are the folks who can exist without some kind of artificial stimulation. While hiking the famous Appalachian Trail, I've even known people who climbed to the top of a mountain and were thrilled when they heard what kind of enhanced reception they could get on their phones.

You just can't develop a deep spiritual life under those conditions. I have learned first-hand that it takes weeks and months of solitude and quiet before you can even begin to slow down enough to connect with your inner voices.

This realization gives us some insight into the contrast in the Robin Hood sagas between the metaphorical villains of the city and the heroes of the wilderness. One is a place of striving and ego-driven ambition. The other is a place of natural rhythms conducive to spiritual contentment.

Remember that we are talking about symbolism here, within the context of a myth. I'm not siding with those who think that the wilderness is some kind of pristine environment wherein only happiness and contentment abide. All the pictures you see that feature vistas, trees, and water don't usually feature mosquitoes and black flies.

Jean-Jacques Rousseau once said that "Man is born free but is everywhere in chains." These were the opening lines to his powerful work, *The Social Contract*, which argued that man is born naturally good but becomes corrupted by civilized society and human institutions. He believed, or at least wrote, that we have to improve our lot in life by returning to nature and living a slower-paced life, at peace with our neighbors.

He was right, I think, but a bit simplistic. It takes more than that. He was a proponent of democracy. But his work more than hints at a form of egalitarianism.

I once attended a state-wide church gathering centered around the theme of environmentalism. It was a well-organized retreat, held in a beautiful church built right on the Gulf of Mexico, in Florida. It was attended primarily by upper-middle-class nature lovers who wouldn't even think of throwing a soda can out the window.

But I was troubled throughout the entire weekend. The bulk of the people at that meeting were what I privately call "greenhouse" ecologists. That term requires some explanation.

I have been an outdoorsman most of my adult life. When I was a little younger, I would habitually take as long as a week off, in both spring and fall, to go into the woods and live off the land. I mean that very literally. I wouldn't take any food with me. All I had was a rifle or bow and arrow, perhaps a fishing rod, a hunting knife and a sleeping bag or blanket. I would forage for my food and if I couldn't hunt, gather, or fish up some supper I went hungry. Some of the best spiritual moments of my life were spent eating roast woodchuck cooked over an open fire, and served up with some roots or berries accompanied by pine needle tea laced with wild mint. I have experienced the sublime, but also know firsthand about things like mosquitoes and black flies. The great outdoors is a beautiful place, but I think we ought to find the guy who invented the screened-in porch and award him the Nobel Prize. I have donated lots of money to groups ranging from the Sierra Club to Ducks Unlimited and have volunteered many, many hours to the Appalachian Trail Club and local outdoors organizations. When I talk about ecology and the beauty of God in nature, I speak from an intimate knowledge and a lot of experience spent actually living outdoors.

This brings us to "greenhouse" ecologists. Because of all the gardening I've done, I have learned about hardening off plants before they can be placed outside. When you start tomato seedlings, for instance, from seed in the greenhouse, they look beautiful and prolific as long as they remain in their controlled environment. But if you take them right outside and plant them in the garden, exposed to the sun, wind, rain, heat, cold, and draught, they wilt and, usually, die. The real outdoors is too much for them. They simply can't take it. They need to experience the wild outdoors in small doses before they are ready.

People are like that. We love the outdoors as long as we stand in climate-controlled comfort and look at it through a window. But to actually walk out into a range of dessert mountains or canoe into a mosquito infested swamp? That's another story! Our so-called "primitive" ancestors had the skills. We don't. This is the twenty-first century. Most people just don't have that kind of experience to draw on. A large part of urban America frames ecological issues in a completely different way than those of us whose understanding of backcountry is forged well away from maintained trails and officially sanctioned campgrounds.

All this was rumbling about in my mind that weekend as I entered a beautiful church, full of the latest technology, that stood about one hundred yards from a beautiful beach located right on the Gulf of Mexico. We saw a gorgeous Power Point presentation featuring pictures of planet Earth. The music consisted of aboriginal flutes and synthesized strings, earth drums and midi-track percussion. As the light dimmed for the production, I became aware that we were most definitely meeting in a church sanctuary. "Sanctuary" means a place of refuge. It consists of safe, secure, surrounding walls. Even the light was filtered by beautiful stained-glass windows. No natural light for us! The only complaint people had was that the air conditioning made the place a little cool. Some people felt the need for a light sweater.

As picture morphed into picture, we learned about the necessity to do two things. First of all, we needed to love, protect, and care for Mother Earth. Second, we needed to spread the word to others. Remember those two things. They will come back to haunt us in a few paragraphs.

One way, we were told, to experience the great outdoors that was being ravaged by development even as we met, was to perform an elaborate ritual in our churches. It consisted of obtaining sawdust from a local building supply store and bringing it home to our congregations, along with sheets of plastic and biodegradable paint. Then we were taught how to make what was, in effect, a copy of a Navaho sand painting. Young and old could be involved in planning the design, painting it on the sawdust which was spread on the plastic sheet, and then dancing together in celebratory mourning for the loss of trees and the natural world when developers raise their ugly heads. The dancing, of course, ruined the painting, so after the ritual was complete, we were all instructed to gather up the sawdust, take it home, and use it as mulch for our gardens.

My wife and I just looked at each other in disbelief. We didn't know whether to laugh or cry. We were sitting in an air-conditioned sanctuary, cut off by four walls that eliminated everything natural, looking at plastic flowers on the walls, and listening to digitized music while looking at pictures of Mother Earth. Filtered air, filtered light, filtered music, and enhanced pictures. The ritual we were taught, which was to help celebrate nature, consisted of plastic sheets, construction wastes, and chemically treated paint. Fossil fuels galore had been burned up in driving to this event. And the service ended with the singing of a hymn extolling the fact that this is God's world.

That night we took a walk on the beach rather than attend the evening workshops. The Gulf of Mexico was less than a hundred yards away from the front door of the church. When the sun sank into the ocean, I happened to glance up the beach to the north and I was struck by a scene that I will never forget. As far as the eye could see there were people standing quietly, looking in unison toward the west. You could have heard a pin drop. All we heard was the sound of waves and wind. (That is, if we chose to ignore the sound of the traffic on the state highway.) When the sun finally set, without anyone saying "Amen," with no organ postlude and no minister to pronounce a benediction, the beach crowd (pagans all, for a moment, and proud of it!) completed their rite, turned, nodded a few quiet greetings, and slowly went home. We had participated in a ritual as old as the human race. We had experienced beauty and stood in awe and wonder at the riveting sight of unmitigated mystery. We had, together, contemplated the meaning of life. "Beauty is truth, and truth beauty—that is all ye know on earth, and all ye need to know," wrote the English poet John Keats. And the gathered congregation said, each in his or her own way, "Amen!"

The next night, safely ensconced in the cool sanctuary, surrounded by beautiful music and meaningful liturgy, we heard again about the need to experience God in nature and to spread the word to others. For the entire time the service was going on I could think of only one thing. Right outside the door, not one hundred yards away, stood hundreds of people, many of them non-churchgoing people, who were having their own worship service. I wanted to shout at the top of my voice, "Why don't we just open the doors? There's the beauty—the real thing—unfiltered! There are the people! They're only a few steps away!"

But, of course, I'm a well-adjusted, fully accredited, ordained minister. I kept my mouth shut.

The people in that congregation no doubt considered themselves conservationists. And, to a great extent, they were. They wouldn't have been at a meeting like that unless they cared. But their lives were lived on a level of affluence of which former generations could not have even dreamed. Neither Napoleon nor Queen Elizabeth ever kicked back in the evening to watch at their leisure, a Masterpiece Theater rerun. We moderns, however, take such luxuries for granted—so much so that we are hardly aware of the fact that complete climate control is ours at the flick of a switch. What would Peter the Great, in all his regal splendor, have paid for that?

By the same token, the folks out on the beach were probably not aware that a group of people only a few steps away would have welcomed them warmly and delighted in sharing stories of spirituality with them. Many of the beachgoers no doubt had only negative things to say about their previous church experiences. Statistically, any group of people contains a small percentage of those who once felt burned by institutional religion. This group was, no doubt, average.

What if both groups could have reframed their cultural bias to include a healthy respect for their counterparts? Could a bridge have been built between them?

Remember that I am using these two groups as metaphors. I am well aware that there were probably some believers on the beach, as well as pagans in the pews. But when viewed metaphorically, the two groups become a valuable way to picture disparate groups of today's society that have long since given up even the effort to see another point of view. Nevertheless, our spiritual and social health depends on doing just that. We simply must learn to see other points of view while refraining from spiritual pride in our own. It's all about reframing.

What all this tells us is that when we talk about the artificial evils of York and London being separated by the beauties of the natural world in Sherwood Forest, we need to think metaphorically. The Robin Hood sagas are trying to make a point, and they are set in symbolic places that mean something. Prince John and the Sherriff of Nottingham aren't "evil" because they live in a city. And Robin Hood isn't "righteous" because he lives in the wild. Their environment is important because of what it symbolizes, not what it is.

The cities of the story symbolize man-made corruption and greed. The forest symbolizes the natural world from whence we sprang.

The message then becomes a simple one. When we lose our way and fall victim to human-created, ego-driven, norms and customs, one way out is to defy it all, and symbolically move outside the system. We don't need to cheat to get ahead just because everyone else seems to be doing it. We can live honest lives even if it means we will never get rewarded. We can do the right things because they are right, not because they are expedient. We can ignore those things which assault our senses and, in the words of the mythologist Joseph Campbell, we can choose to "follow our bliss."

This is the path of Robin Hood. Not the historical man, if he ever even existed. But the mythological hero. His story speaks to us today in constantly fresh and evolving concepts, changing to meet the needs of every new generation.

When the city throws us out, the wilderness is still there to receive us. All we need do is find our own Sherwood Forest. If we open our eyes, Robin will find us and show us the way.

Part II: The Hero

A hero ventures forth from the world of common day into a region of supernatural wonder: fabulous forces are there encountered and a decisive victory is won: the hero comes back from this mysterious adventure with the power to bestow boons on his fellow man.

(Joseph Campbell in *The Hero with a Thousand Faces*)

In 1949, Joseph Campbell, a professor of mythology at Sarah Lawrence College, published his first book, *The Hero with a Thousand Faces*. He received an advance of $750 from his publisher, Pantheon Books. His thesis was that there is a typical mythological motif that is repeated over and over again in many forms of oral history, literature, and legend, but the story is always the same. An unsuspecting, seemingly every-day-type person is somehow transported out of his mundane existence, goes on an adventure, and comes back a hero, who is able to bring a gift to humanity as a result of lessons learned on his journey. It became one of those books that for many years never sold very well, but the right people seemed to read it and quietly pass it along to others.

One of those who received a copy was George Lucas, who later said that if he had never read it, he could never have written and produced the movie, *Star Wars*. When that fact became evident to journalist and political commentator Bill Moyers, he interviewed Campbell for the 1988 six-part PBS documentary, *The Power of Myth*. The series soon became one of the most popular shows in the history of American public television. It made Joseph Campbell, who had by then retired from teaching, a household name, and introduced the concepts of "follow your bliss" and "the hero's journey" to a huge popular audience.

Campbell confessed that one of his own heroes was Douglas Fairbanks, who had starred in the swashbuckling silent adventure film, *Douglas Fairbanks in Robin Hood*. It was the first motion picture to have ever had a Hollywood premiere, which was held at Grauman's Egyptian Theater on October 18, 1922. It was one of the most expensive films of the 1920s, with a budget of some one million dollars, but it was big hit and received mostly favorable reviews. Those that were unfavorable generally commented on the fact that making such movies was never going to amount to anything and was a waste of money.

Since then, more than fifty actors have brought Robin Hood to the big screen, including such luminaries as Kevin Costner, Russell Crowe, Erroll Flynn, Sean Connery, Richard Greene, George Segal, and Patrick Bergin. Robin has become the hero who will never die. His story lives on, changing and evolving each time with the telling.

Every version of his story has him doing different things at different times in history. Sometimes he helps bring about the signing of the Magna Carta, the document reluctantly signed by the tremendously unpopular King John at Runnymede in 1215. It promised protection of church rights, protection against illegal imprisonment, access to swift justice, and limitations of payments to the Crown.

Other versions of Robin's story have him going off to the Crusades with good King Richard. Upon his return, he discovers his lands and titles have been confiscated by the evil Prince John, and he is forced to take up an outlaw life in Sherwood Forest.

But the version that has stood the test of time is the one that forms the basis for the ballads, the songs of the troubadours. These are the songs that tell the well-known stories that form the basis for the larger-than-life tales of Robin slowly collecting his band of Merry Men: Little John and the famous quarter staff fight on the bridge, wherein Robin is bested by the one who will soon become his second in command, Friar Tuck and the incident at the river crossing, Will Scarlett, Maid Marian, and all the rest. Most of these came about after the medieval time, but there is a core sampling that scholars attribute to the early days of the era: *Robin Hood and the Monk, Robin Hood and Guy of Gisborne, Robin Hood and the Potter*, and the *Lytyll Geste of Robin Hode*, are a few of them.

This last is probably the most important collection. *A Gest of Robin Hode* was printed shortly after 1500, but the stories are probably older than that, dating to possibly as early as the mid-1300s. This would place it within a hundred years of the events it claims to present. To put this in perspective, many biblical texts were written at least this long after the events they portray, so we can't judge the documents too harshly.

Robin Hood presents the classic hero's myth that Joseph Campbell wrote about. He is a man who, through no fault of his own, was transported out of the life he was leading. He encountered villains and beasts, escaped many a trap by the skin of his teeth, rose victorious from the fray, and then returned, having defeated his foes and rescued the maiden fair. He didn't blow up the Death Star, like Luke Skywalker, but he accomplished everything else a real hero was expected to do. At the end, with the return of King Richard, he was rewarded and, presumably, lived happily ever after.

The story is such a fine example of the hero's journey that it continues to stand the test of time. His triumphant style, his good-natured attitude in the face of danger, his courage, his skill, and his humanity shine through his every deed.

For these reasons he is a legend, and will continue to be for many generations to come. But the symbolism that permeates his story is what we will look at in the following pages, because more than being simply an exciting hero, the nature of his adventures, and those of the people he gathered around him, have a lot to teach us about how to overcome adversity in our own lives. The troubadours were well aware of this, and crafted their accounts accordingly.

As a result, Robin speaks to the 21st century as well as the 13th.

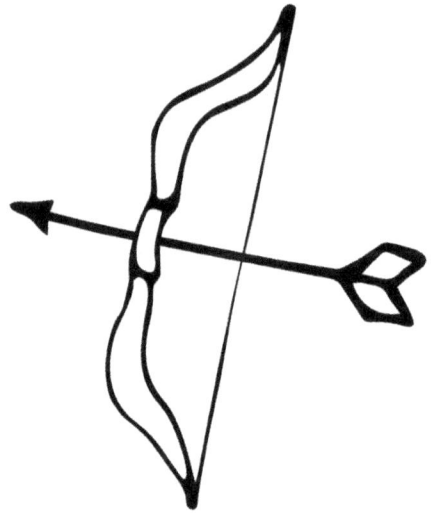

Robin Hood: The Civilized Wild Man

> *COME listen a while, you gentlemen all,*
> *With a hey down down a down down*
> *That are in this bower within,*
> *For a story of gallant bold Robin Hood*
> *I purpose now to begin.*

(*Robin Hood Newly Revived*, from *Child Ballad 128*)

Why does the story of Robin Hood refuse to die? Why doesn't it fade into the background like those of Davy Crockett, Zorro, and other legends who had their day in the sun and then became only a pleasant memory? Why are movies still made and books written? Why does the television's History Channel still feature documentaries in search of the "real" Robin Hood?

It might have something to do with a deeply ingrained search for what real masculinity encompasses in a world that often features confusing, and even contradictory, expectations about what it means to be a modern man.

To understand how this came about, especially in western cultures, we need look no further than what happened in America following World War II. Men had come back from Europe and the South Pacific to a hero's welcome. They were treated as returning warriors who had won a global conflict. A real man stood tall in battle for a noble cause, and was treated as such.

But something happened in the years that followed. First in Korea, and then in Vietnam, the role of a warrior began to undergo a sea change in popular opinion. Where young men had once run out to sign up after Pearl Harbor, answering the call that trumpeted "Uncle Sam Needs You!", they now began to burn their draft cards and shout, "Hell no, I won't go!"

College campuses became hotbeds of a liberal mindset that questioned traditional male values. The burgeoning feminist movement obliterated the idea that men were supposed to be in charge while "the little woman" stayed home, raised babies, and tended the house. Young men began to treat women differently. It became important to listen with empathy and try to understand the arguments of others. In many circles, "real men" became gentle and caring, sharing and compassionate. These were attributes John Wayne rarely personified in movies wherein arguments were settled at the point of a gun.

By the 1970s, and into the 1980s, men's groups were formed so that men could face a changing climate of understanding. What did it mean to be a real man? What did a real man even look like? Did he have to be a large, physical specimen who played on the football team? Or could women fall for the captain of the chess club? Brains or brawn? Which was it?

Perhaps the whole situation came to a head in the summer of 1984. Two men went on a summer-long concert tour, each with his own brand of music. Both tours were considered a success, but it was obvious that their fans were beginning to polarize. They liked either one or the other, but seldom both.

Michael Jackson went out on what was called the Victory Tour. His studio album, *Thriller*, was a monster hit, and the stage show he put together to accompany it was epic.

Meanwhile, Bruce Springsteen had his own hit with *Born in the USA*. His show didn't feature moon-walking and practiced dance moves. It was just straight-ahead rock and roll, forthright and in-your-face.

Springsteen was obviously built to last. He was "The Boss!" A man's man all the way. Michael? Well, he tried to pull off some macho moves and affected all the right postures and poses. But somehow it seemed as though a good wind could blow him off stage. He was a little too full of himself. Talented? Immensely! But between he and Springsteen, who hailed from the streets of New Jersey, there was no doubt who seemed more masculine.

By 1990, the whole masculine image was ready for a remake. It came about because of a poet named Robert Bly. His self-help bestseller, *Iron John*, hit a nerve in an American public who was confused about the whole changing role of what it means to be a modern man.

Iron John was an exegesis of Jacob and Wilhelm Grimm's tale of *Iron Hans*, a story about what it means to be a man. It's a coming-of-age tale, involving a young man and his mentor. Bly had been delivering talks and lecturing about mythology, largely to supplement his income. He discovered that when he talked about *Iron John*, men sat up and listened.

In order to bring the story home and make it meaningful, he had given his audience a visual aid that involved re-enacting a scene from the *Odyssey*. In Homer's ancient epic, Odysseus had been instructed to raise his sword against Circe, the manifestation of female energy. But Bly discovered that many young men who had come of age during the Vietnam war wanted nothing to do with a manhood that could only express itself by having an enemy. These men were open and receptive to different viewpoints, as opposed to the "my way or the highway" model that often dominated the masculine landscape of their fathers.

Bly called such men "soft males," but in no way implied they were weak or less manly. Indeed, he taught that the world was a much better place because of their presence. Harmony and balance do not necessarily translate to passivity and weakness, but when men felt these feelings, they often considered themselves failures. He discouraged this kind of thinking, but at the same time tried to teach them that flashing swords had a place in the great scheme of things. There was a time to wage war, and a time to make peace. There is a time for battle, and a time for what he called "joyful decisiveness."

In short, through *Iron John*, Robert Bly tried, through poetry, myth, the beating of drums, the sharing of personal stories, and even, yes, tree-hugging, to lead men back to the source of their masculinity. In a significant application of the teaching of the Buddha, Bly tried to teach men to find a middle way between what he called "the sensitive, new-age guy" and the power and vitality of the warrior. It was no accident, he said over and over again, that the brothers Grimm had originally included a shorter version of this tale in their 1815 book of fairytales. But there it was called, in German, *De wilde Mann* ("The Wild Man.")

In this version, a "civilized" young man risks all and enters the forest with "the wild man," who becomes his mentor. His parents think he has been seduced and captured by the devil, but in reality, he is about to discover how to merge his inner wildness with his inner, civilized, self. It's a story about initiation and awakening. Bly's message was that what had become the modern obsession with making childhood, in his words, "a cocoon of light," closes off young boys to a real source of power. Psychologists had begun to call this "the dark side," and it was seen as something to be eliminated by schools, for instance, that taught boys to sit in straight rows, talk and act a certain way, and generally fall in line. Harmony and higher consciousness, he believed, can hold a certain attraction to young, naïve men. By adopting such thoughts without understanding them, they can lose something very important—their "wildness."

The way through, he taught, was to undergo the equivalent of a quest to find the essential nature of what it means to be a balanced man in the image of the heroes of mythology—Odysseus, for example, who could fight with the best of them, yet still cook and clean the house without feeling he was doing "woman's work."

If warrior energy is not honored and channeled, it expresses itself in unhealthy ways. Young men join gangs, for instance, or beat their wives, or bully others. A starched uniform and a chest full of medals represents the civilizing of warrior energy. But there are other ways. A real man, according to Bly's teaching, has tamed his wildness without sublimating it. He *uses* it rather than *exploits* it.

Robin Hood is the personification of the civilized wild man. He is masculine without being overbearing. He stands up to corrupt authority, but honors the real king. He takes the ill-gotten riches of those who subjugate the poor, and redistributes the wealth in a fair and equitable fashion. He is a man's man who is not a threat to women. He is a devout Christian who recognizes the rot in his church's hierarchy, and seeks to root it out. He gathers around him a band of men who want to emulate him. He is a natural leader. He is a hero. And he does it all with humor and good will. That's why his story endures to this day.

Part III: The Antagonists

an·tag·o·nist – noun:
A person who actively opposes or is hostile to someone or something; an adversary.

(Merriam-Webster Dictionary)

We usually experience our world in terms of duality, or pairs of opposites. It's a simplistic view of life, but one that works. When we think up/down, cold/hot, right/wrong, and left/right, it usually serves us well. The problem comes when we apply the experience of duality to complex issues that have more than two sides to them. The evening news, for instance, often claims to present "both sides" of a story. But social issues rarely have only two sides. And there is real danger to reducing relationships to "us" and "them," or, even worse, "us" *against* "them." In war, for example, there are always individual "thems" that don't agree with their leadership.

When we dropped atomic weapons on Japan, for instance, we justified the killing of thousands of innocent victims who had committed no crimes other than being born Japanese, on the grounds that it was "us" against "them." That's what war does.

During the American Civil War, when General William Tecumseh Sherman vowed to end the conflict by taking the battle to the civilian population of Georgia because "they" were supporting the war effort, he was perceived as a hero in the north and a villain in the south.

Undoubtedly both the atomic bombs dropped on Japan and Sherman's march to the sea ended the respective conflicts and probably saved lives. But the issue was far more complex than a simple "us against them" argument.

That's a problem with stories about heroes. For every hero, there is an antagonist. Good guys/bad guys, cowboys/Indians, and cops/robbers make for straight forward, simplistic story-telling, but the outcomes can have far-reaching, multi-generational consequences.

I was once personally called on, in my capacity as the pastor of a church, to help reconcile two men who were feuding because one of them bought a Volkswagen too soon after World War II. It wasn't a pleasant experience.

What this means is that when we read about Robin Hood, Prince John, and the Sherriff of Nottingham, we need to, once more, think in terms of metaphors. What's important is that which the characters represent, not who they are in a historical sense.

This is complicated because Prince John *was* a historical character who was hated during his lifetime, and the sheriff could be based on a real person as well. So, we have to carefully decide to treat them, at least in terms of the Robin Hood story, as *symbolic* antagonists, put in place to give Robin, the protagonist hero of the tale, a convenient foil, remembering that no one is either as perfectly good or perfectly bad as they are presented in legend.

Generally speaking, in all literature, including the Robin Hood sagas, antagonists can be divided into four basic groups:

- Villains: These are the traditional "bad guys" who are set up to give the hero his or her chance to triumph. For every Luke Skywalker there is a Darth Vader. For every Harry Potter there needs to be a Lord Voldemort.

- Conflict-Creators: These antagonists are not necessarily "bad" in the classic sense. In Victor's Hugo's *Les Misérables,* for instance, Javert is not a "bad guy" for trying to arrest Valjean. He's just a cop trying to do his duty, misguided though it may be.

- Inanimate Forces: Sometimes the antagonist can be something as innocuous as bad weather causing a storm at sea, or a snow storm that forces a hero to persevere through unfavorable and dangerous elements.

- Inner Demons: When I first read J.D. Salinger's *The Catcher in the Rye*, I was a teenager, new to literature. But even then, I was struck by the fact that Holden Caulfield was his own worst enemy.

In the case of Robin Hood, the antagonists most definitely fall into the "Villain" category. But they are villains of a particular type. Their villainy stems from the fact that they are driven by narcissism which at least borders on psychopathology.

Narcissists generally feel entitled and grandiose. They are at the center not only of their own story, but everyone else's. They usually lack any real empathy, and are arrogant as well. They are normally in search of validation, but they might feel at least a small sense of shame when they do wrong, if only because getting caught undermines their self-esteem.

A psychopath, on the other hand, doesn't feel any shame. That's why they can generally pass lie-detector tests. They honestly feel they can do no wrong because they are the ones performing the deeds. If they do something, it is obviously justified, because they are the ones doing it.

In the case of Robin Hood, his antagonists are pretty close to being psychopaths—narcissists on steroids—ego run amuck. In this story, we once again face the constant problem of how to react to ego's seemingly eternal struggle for dominance, both in Robin's world, and, by extension, ours.

In stories such as the fable of Little Snow-White, the protagonist conquers through her innocence. In the case of someone like Merlin the Magician, he battles ego through earth magic left over from a forgotten time. In the story of Robin Hood, he defies ego simply by being a hero. His character is such that he refuses to bow down to ego in any form, and, using only his own skill and personality, triumphs in the end.

In a day and age such as ours, with narcissistic ego on the rise in every arena from politics to religion, from academia to science, in the world of the office and marketplace, on stage and in sports stadiums, it is important for us to think, and think seriously, about how we are going to live our lives. Technology and the Internet have made it very easy for everyone to project themselves into the public arena, presenting themselves as larger-than-life figures who know much more than they really do. Everyone, it seems, is an "expert" nowadays, eager to inflict their own brand of ego on anyone who will listen.

Perhaps Robin Hood can teach us how to defy such people, honorably and with joyful gusto. His story is inspirational, as well as instructive

With that as an introduction, let's study his antagonists. Chances are good that you will recognize their characters right away. You've certainly seen them on TV.

Maybe you even work with a few of them, but here's hoping you're not related to them. What do you think? Let's see.

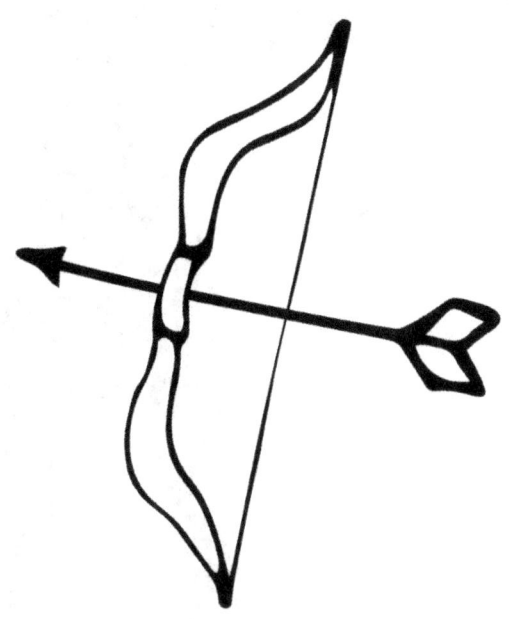

Prince John: The Usurper

Oh, the world will sing of an English King
A thousand years from now
And not because he passed some laws
Or had that lofty brow
While bonny good King Richard leads
The great crusade he's on
We'll all have to slave away
For that good-for-nothin' John
Incredible as he is inept
Whenever the history books are kept
They'll call him the phony king of England
[Chorus:] A pox on the phony king of England!

(From *Robin Hood*, lyrics by Johnny Mercer)

The story of the English monarchy is convoluted and tough to follow. Although we're looking at the tale of Robin Hood through the eyes of metaphor and symbolism, even the waters of this approach are a bit muddied, because some of the characters, if not Robin himself, are real, historical figures.

Take "Good King Richard," for instance. That's how he is usually referred to in the sagas, but history has quite a different view of him. He is called "Richard the Lionheart" and the "Crusader King," but he barely spent any time in England at all. His mother was Eleanor of Aquitaine, the Queen of France. His father was King Henry II, of the Plantagenet royal house, which originated in the lands of Anjou in France. It's clear that he considered the heart of his kingdom to be in France, although his family held the English throne for more than three hundred years and undoubtedly transformed the British Isles.

20th century historians are not as kind to him as their earlier colleagues. He didn't seem to care very much about the responsibility of leadership and the health of his kingdom. His decisions were superficial rather than well thought out. Given his seeming lack of interest in women, some even believe that he was bisexual, or even gay. (Not, as Jerry Seinfeld reminded us on his TV show, that there's anything wrong with that!) But his lack of interest in

England makes us wonder why he was referred to as a "good" King.

So why does he get such good press in the ballads? The answer is simple. Being concerned with his press clippings, so to speak, and his reputation, he was a great patron of the arts—meaning he supported troubadours and bards. And who wrote the Robin Hood ballads? Troubadours and bards! His good reputation in the popular "press," so to speak, is probably as obvious as that. The ones who gave us Robin Hood knew what side their bread was buttered on, and who buttered it.

Richard's younger brother, Prince John, was also a historical figure. But he was never referred to as "good," even by later historians who had no patron to appease. There is no question that when Richard left to go crusading, John tried to usurp the throne for himself. Indeed, although he ruled as King John from 1199 to 1216, his reputation, both political and personal, is anything but exemplar. He is considered to be one of the worst kings in England's long history of questionable rulers. He lost the Plantagenet lands in France, and financially crippled England in order to pay for his fiasco. The barons finally rebelled and forced him to sign the Magna Carta in 1215, in which he gave up most of his royal power. That historic document is famous for limiting the absolute rule of royalty in favor of the rule of law, and marks the beginning of a long and bloody path toward the constitutional monarchy England enjoys today.

But while all this was developing, Robin Hood enters the picture. John is still a prince during the time of which the ballads sing. He's not yet a king. But Robin's penchant for stealing from the rich and giving to the poor is a direct result of the troubadour's editorializing John's greed and lust for wealth. Taxes were high, often outlandish, and punishment for non-payment was severe. It is no wonder the people needed to hear songs about a hero who championed them in their plight.

Things came to a head when Richard was captured on his way home from the Third Crusade, and held for ransom by the Holy Roman Empire. John was good at fund raising, to say the least. He saw this as an opportunity to raise money, ostensibly for the ransom payment, but his plan was to steal both the money and the throne.

The plot was thwarted, but John was extremely deceptive. When Richard finally returned briefly to

England in 1194, he forgave his brother for his excessive ambition, and went so far as to nominate him his successor. When Richard died in battle during the siege of Chalus, on April 6, 1199, John became King of England, and was duly crowned the very next month at Westminster Abbey.

Even though John was a real, historical figure, albeit a terrible king, the name most often associated with him is that of a (probably) fictional character named Robin Hood. It seems obvious, then, that the real Prince John was paired with a fictional Robin Hood so as to serve as a foil for the name that was about to become a legend.

The common man was, for the most part, powerless in those days. Even more so was the common woman. So the hero, Robin, was usually pictured with a yeoman's bow and arrow, rather than the sword of a medieval knight or nobleman. Through no fault of his own, Robin was ostracized and declared an outlaw. This would have resonated with the typical peasant. They could only imagine living a free life, ignoring the burden of taxes and laws.

The stories were written beginning in the 14th century, not the late 11th and early 12th in which they were set. That accounts for the rather untrustworthy historical accuracy. They portray an imagined memory, not history.

But that, in itself, tells us a lot. They were meant to be received as metaphor and symbolism. What was important was not who the characters *were*. It is what they *meant*. Robin was of noble birth, like Richard, but the evil Prince John tried to drive him out and away from his heritage, just as he did with regards to his brother, Richard.

It is possible that this was an addition meant to mollify the aristocracy of later centuries, who were probably somewhat averse to a commoner being made into such a hero. They might well have influenced the bards to make Robin one of their own, albeit mightily wronged, in order to save face.

But what does that have to do with today's recipients of the story? What does Robin have to teach us?

We are all familiar with politicians of every stripe—presidents, governors, mayors, and local officials—who are more interested in the power and influence of their job than the service it entails. Too often, election to one office simply serves as a stepping stone to the one above it, even if that means usurping a superior's position when he or she is away doing something else.

Richard was away at the Crusades, rather than doing his job at home. John took advantage of the fact. That happens everywhere. Politicians take advantage of even desperate situations, using them as an excuse to raise funds, just as John did when Richard was being ransomed. Then the funds are syphoned off for private purposes. It's a situation that is only too familiar nowadays.

At such times we all, feeling powerless, look around to see if we can find a hero like Robin Hood. So it becomes advantageous to study what he did, and how he reacted to the situation. Perhaps there are some universal lessons to learn in this case. Robin might be able to teach us a thing or two.

Lesson #1: Be true to your values

According to the ballads, Robin, who justifiably could have been forgiven for being bitter about losing his lands, his income, his title, and his reputation, never indulged in self-pity. Never do we read about a woe-is-me moment wherein he blamed ill fortune, bad luck, or cosmic forces for his lot in life. Never did he ask, "Why does this kind of thing always happen to me?"

Instead, he accepted the injustice of it all, rode with the punches, and went about making the best of a difficult situation. If ever there is a case in literature where the expression, "If life hands you lemons, make lemonade" applies, it is right here. Robin wasted no time feeling sorry for himself. Instead, he looked around, decided on a course of action, and took it. He didn't look back. He looked ahead, with cheerful determination and up-beat attitude. He is always pictured laughing, not moping. Even as he engages in battle, there is a smile on his face.

Bad things happen to good people. That is simply the way life works. Sometimes it seems as though the universe in conspiring against us. But the universe doesn't play favorites. It is a universal, neutral stage upon which we actors play our part. When the play is over and the curtain rings down, we exit the stage and go back where we came from. Sometimes the play is a comedy. Sometimes it's a tragedy. But eventually it is over, and what matters is not whether the audience laughs or cries when the lights come back on, it's how well we played our role. In the theater, when it comes time for the final round of applause, even the villain, after he puts aside the role he was playing and comes out on stage as his real self, gets applauded, *if* he acted his part with sincerity and skill.

Robin Hood teaches us how to roll with the punches while demonstrating good will and positive mental attitude.

In 2014, The New England Patriots football team was struggling early in the season. Things came to a head when the team was blown out by the Kansas City Chiefs by a score of 41 to 14. Even before the game was over, commentators we're saying that the Patriots were "done." Their dynasty was over. Their quarterback was too old, and he was over the hill. The coach had lost his ability to lead. After only five games into the season, there was no longer any reason to continue.

Following the loss, Coach Bill Belichick appeared at the post-game news conference and said the now-famous words, "We're on to Cincinnati." The press pushed him to talk about the loss they had just endured. Again, he said, "We're on to Cincinnati." Reporters wouldn't settle for that. It seemed too simplistic. Five times they pushed him.

Five times he said, in effect, "we're not looking back. That's over. We're looking ahead." He was roundly laughed at that week, and ridiculed. Even so, the Patriots pushed on, doing what they always did, concentrating on their long-range plan, which was based on a short-range idiom, "Do your job."

That phrase became the title of an NFL special documentary, *Do Your Job: Bill Belichick and the 2014 Patriots*, after New England went on to win the Superbowl in spectacular fashion that season.

Later, after the smoke had cleared on that eventful time, Belichick was asked why he made his famous speech which said, in essence, that he wasn't going to look back, but rather ahead. "I could have said it three times, I could have said it 53 times. It could have been 103 times, if that's what they wanted to keep asking, because we had to turn the page," he said.

Belichick, like Robin Hood, refused to whine and mope about loss. Instead, he believed in what he was doing, and moved forward. He remained true to himself and his values.

Lesson #2: Keep up a good humor

It's hard to move forward in a positive way while feeling down in the dumps and sorry for yourself. One of the things that drew me to the Robin Hood story when I was young was the fact that there always seemed to be a healthy positive attitude about my hero. Even when Little John was knocking him off a bridge, or Friar Tuck was tossing him into a river, he was able to laugh at himself. That's a valuable lesson for a young boy to learn. I wish I had applied it more through the years, but at least I was aware of it during those times in my adult life when life seemed overwhelming.

I'm older now, and well into the inevitable process of staring death in the face. The temptation, and I freely confess I give in to it way too often, is to look back at all the mistakes I made during my life, instead of the successes. It's hard to smile when the metaphorical Prince John, in the guise of aging muscles, failing sight and hearing, loss of energy, and general malaise, rob me of what I consider to be my "rightful" lands and titles of youthful health and strength. Like Robin, I face the challenge of loss. Unlike him, I rarely do it with a smile on my lips.

Lesson #3: Gather a support group of trustworthy allies

This is a tough one. There would be no Robin Hood stories without the Merry Men. They are an integral part of the ballads. Robin didn't go it alone.

But it's hard to find such support these days. We are a culture prone to look out for #1, and most people participate in a group because of what they can get out of it. Selfishness and ego do not exist only in the camp of the bad guys, such as those who followed Prince John. Chances are good that you have experienced the pain of feeling the need to be supported, only to have the ones you trusted turn around and cry on your shoulder instead.

Remember that this is a story, not a history lesson, so Robin was lucky in his choice of companions. You might not be quite as fortunate. But the principle is still important. A good-hearted person generally attracts good-hearted companions. Losers usually attract losers. A positive personality gathers positivity. Whiners clump together as well.

We have to ask ourselves what we are going to do in order to manifest positivity. That is easier said than done. But it's important to at least recognize the reality. The ballads do just that.

In a few pages we will begin to examine the types of personalities Robin Hood drew to himself. But for now, we need to at least file away an important truth. It's important to recognize the place ego plays in our lives. It can be a positive force for success, propelling us forward, or a negative force for failure, holding us back. What happens is usually out of our control. How we react to what happens is entirely in our own hands.

This, then, is the first of Robin's antagonists. Prince John, the Usurper, represents the impersonal forces of ego run amuck. Robin doesn't see him very often. He is "out there," issuing orders that affect common people, just as politicians, presidents, heads of huge corporations, and various captains of industry affect us every day. We don't see them, but we suffer injustice when their decisions filter down through the chains of economic, spiritual, and political commands.

A top executive, a member of Congress, or even a Supreme Court justice, are part of a patriarchal system of government that is all too common throughout history. Any of them can issue a decree that affects us adversely. We might not ever meet them in person, but we feel the effects of what they decide. Down through the ages, rich and powerful people have, just like Prince John, found ways to increase their power and wealth at the expense of the poor. That is a fact of life.

Sometimes, people at the top seem beyond our reach, especially if we live in a country without free and fair elections, our only source of political clout. But they usually have people down the line who are closer to us, people we interact with on a daily basis, who carry out the orders of their superiors. These are a second category of antagonists.

Such a person was one of Robin's immediate adversaries. He is known as the Sheriff of Nottingham.

The Sheriff of Nottingham:
The Patriarchy's Political Puppet

Syr sheryffe for thy sake
Robyn hode wull y take.
I wyll the gyffe golde and fee
This be heste þu holde me.
Robyn hode ffayre and fre
vndre this lynde shote we.
with the shote y wyll
Alle thy lustes to full fyll.

(Transcribed from Cambridge, Trinity College MS R.2.64 [fragment], c. 1475)

When it comes to the antagonists found within the pages of the Robin Hood sagas, the first one to come to mind is undoubtedly the Sheriff of Nottingham. He is usually pictured as a kind of slimy villain who schemed his way to the top.

In the movies, Alan Rickman best personified the most essentially evil character of them all, but that is to be expected. After all, Rickman will be forever remembered as Severus Snape of Harry Potter fame. Add to that his roles as the bad guy in the 1988 movie, *Die Hard,* and the 1990 film, *Quigley Down Under*, and it's hard to imagine better type-casting.

In the ballads, as in life, the sheriff is the one who carries out the will of his superiors. Prince John issues the actual decrees, but he's off in his castle somewhere. It's the sheriff who does the dirty work. That's the way governments work. So, the Sheriff is the one Robin actually has to deal with.

That raises a bit of a problem for those who are still looking for historical accuracy, because there was no sheriff in the town of Nottingham until 1449. That was more than two hundred years after the times in which the stories are set, and a good seventy years after they were first written down.

But have no fear. History offers us an out. Even though the town didn't have a sheriff, the shire of Nottinghamshire did, and probably a few people referred to him as the Sheriff of Nottingham. We can take comfort in that.

He would have been sheriff of not only Nottingham, but neighboring Derbyshire as well. In 1189, records show that Prince John appointed a "reeve," an official something like a sheriff, to hold down the responsibilities that a sheriff would have. So that offers a bit of historical flavor.

It was the custom in those days for the sheriffs to carry the burden for the taxes incurred by the towns or shires they served. They, in turn, collected from the people. A system like that invites the local sheriff to collect a good deal for himself, as well as that which he passes on to the king. If the sheriff didn't make the payments, he lost his job.

In 1204, King John passed a law saying that the sheriffs were not expected to keep any of the county's revenues. That didn't carry any weight, or course, because sheriffs weren't in the habit of reporting how much they collected. There were no checks or balances. So all the law accomplished was to let John off the hook. He could claim innocence while the local officials stole from their people.

Most of the money collected was probably in the forms of bribes anyway, so it never appeared in the official registers.

In 1170, Henry II led an inquest which was said to make the local sheriffs "professional administrators." King John did something similar in 1213. But rumors about corrupt sheriffs fill the official records for years after that, so it's safe to say that the whole system of corrupt sheriffs probably led to the invention of the Sheriff of Nottingham being Robin Hood's chief antagonist and adversary. Every hero needs someone to triumph over, and Robin is no exception.

So, as we have been doing throughout this book, let's not look too much into who the Sheriff might have been, but rather what kind of role he plays in the story as a literary character, rather than a historical figure.

To do that we have to ask a question. Who is the worst villain? The one who gives an immoral edict? Or the one who carries it out?

Look, for instance, at the terrible time we now call the Spanish Inquisition of the Roman Catholic Church, beginning in 1478.

Its official title was the Tribunal of the Holy Office of the Inquisition, proposed and ordered by King Ferdinand II of Aragorn and Queen Isabella I of Castile. It stated that anyone who disagreed with church doctrine was in danger of being turned over to the authorities of the church, who also held sway over the political establishment.

The Inquisition had a unique method of operation. First, the defendant was declared guilty by the local Bishops and church hierarchy. Then came the trial, the only purpose of which was to give the guilty party a chance to recant. Often, this second phase was accompanied by fiendish torture that led to death. If the victim recanted, he, or, in a few cases, she, was still killed. But at least, so it was thought, they had the solace of knowing they would be divinely pardoned and could still enter heaven after appropriate fees had been paid by their relatives and loved ones.

The question, then, is this. Who was most responsible for the evil perpetrated during those days? Was it the monarchs who initiated the process? Or was it the Bishops and Inquisitors who carried it out?

Since then, the church has slowly moved to admit its wrongs. The cascading Protestant Reformation, and subsequent internal strife, eventually caused the Inquisition to lose its stranglehold on the population. There were pockets of resistance, of course, and they were not limited to Catholic circles.

In 1692, for instance, more than two hundred people, mostly women, were accused of witchcraft in Salem, Massachusetts. Twenty were executed in the resulting hysteria. Officially, the power behind the trials was the secular state, but it was universally acknowledged that the clergy supported that power. After those trials, closely observed by Cotton Mather, the prominent Puritan preacher, maybe even *because* of those trials, the church lost most of its power to so flagrantly and abusively dominate the population.

Given the sweeping tide of history, church authorities eventually tried to reconcile their errors, but in typical ecclesiastical fashion, it took a while. In 1741 Pope Benedict XIV began the process of apologizing without really admitting to the sin. In 1758 the study of Heliocentrism was removed from the church's famous

Index of Prohibited Books, painting over the disagreements between science and religion that figured so proximately in the purposes behind the Inquisition. In 1990, then Cardinal Ratzinger, who would later become Pope Benedict XVI, recognized that the whole affair was "a symptomatic case that permits us to see how deep the self-doubt of the modern age, of science and technology, goes today," whatever that means.

On October 31, 1992, Pope John Paul II expressed regret for how the whole matter was handled, and confessed to Catholic Church "tribunal errors." But it was a matter of too little, too late, and everybody knew it.

So who was at fault? Using this as an example, Prince John plays the part of the historical Catholic hierarchy. The Sheriff of Nottingham represents the Inquisitors who carried out the process. One issues the orders. The other puts them into effect.

Undoubtedly, both should be blamed. But Prince John was ensconced in his castle. He was hard to reach. The Sheriff, on the other hand, was close at hand, so he is the one who becomes Robin Hood's particular adversary.

Let's apply this to our modern day. Suppose you one day discover that a neighborhood store you have worked with for ages suddenly merges with a conglomerate. New rules are implemented that negatively affect your business dealings. The people who made the decision to merge are anonymous suits in a boardroom located in some big city. You don't even know their names. They are your Prince John, so to speak.

But you *do* know the person in your local store who tells you how things have changed. You have dealt with him or her for years. It's not their fault. They may have had nothing to do with the merger. Maybe they don't even approve of it. But to whom do you vent your frustrations? They become, in effect, your Sheriff of Nottingham.

The same thing happens in war. Americans signed up by the thousands to fight Adolph Hitler. They never saw him. They were never even in his vicinity. But when they aimed their rifles at German soldiers, they were, in effect shooting at him. Hitler, (Prince John) was in Berlin, but, at least in their minds, they aimed at him on the beaches of Normandy and the fields of France when they shot at the proverbial Sheriff of Nottingham.

If the Sheriff had been killed, it would not have changed Robin's lot in life one bit. A new sheriff would have been appointed and things would have continued on as before.

Reading the story in this way, there was a reason Robin didn't simply shoot the sheriff on some of their many escapades. He had plenty of opportunity, but it would have served no purpose. Instead, Robin sought to outwit him, to beat him at his own game.

Lesson #1: Separate symptom from disease

This is a valuable lesson to learn. There is value in fighting the symptoms of a disease. It will make you feel better. That's what Robin did when he confronted the sheriff. But he knew the sheriff was not the real problem. The disease consisted of the actions of Prince John, off in his castle, out of reach. Killing the messenger wouldn't help. It might even make things worse. But at the same time, the messengers must be thwarted as best as we are able. After all, they are spreading the disease.

These days, at least in the United States and most western European countries, political "Prince John" diseases are fought at the ballot box every election year. But that doesn't stop local "Sheriff of Nottingham" politicians from attempting to corrupt the system. The same can said for any private organization that attempt to exploit the public for individual gain.

Usually, the means entail everything from peaceful protests to active boycotts. At least when it comes to dealing with companies. But what if a particular person in an office setting or social situation resorts to bullying or similar tactics?

Robin Hood tells us that there is a time to actively fight back and resist. Every situation is different, so there is no easy answer, but the ballads are full of examples. We'll look at a few of them in the pages to come when we study the exploits of the Merry Men. For now, it's enough to remember that being passive isn't always the right choice.

Lesson #2: However you fight back, do it with joy

The Robin Hood ballads exude joy. Robin is a happy warrior. We never observe him plotting his exploits in a back room somewhere. He and the Merry Men pull off some outlandish stunts, but they are always fun to read about. Not for them are the conspiracy theories and dirty deeds of the counter culture. They enjoy life, and it shows through their every adventure. Often, they even win the trust of those who initially thought them a band of outlaws. Some of the "victims" even join the gang, as was the case with Little John and Friar Tuck.

In today's world, full of dissension and disagreement, it's easy to demonize our opponents. But when we start down that path, it usually leads to our own corruption. Hate affects the hater as well as the one who is hated. If ever there is a literary example of the biblical mandate to "love your enemies," it can be found in the Robin Hood ballads.

Thomas "Tip" O'Neill Jr. represented northern Boston, Massachusetts, as a Democrat elected to the United States House of Representatives, from 1953 to 1987. He served as Speaker of the House from 1977 to 1987. A staunch liberal, close friend to the Kennedy family, and outspoken champion of the so-called "common man," people wondered how he was ever going to work with newly elected president Ronald Regan, who was a darling of the conservatives. The two men seemingly disagreed about everything.

But they became good friends. Why? Regan would stop in to Tip's office, sit down with him, and tell Irish jokes. The two would laugh together, sometimes long into the night. As a result, when they had to disagree about a particular issue, their friendship got them through it.

Robin Hood never became friends with the Sheriff of Nottingham, of course. In the ballads, the sheriff was simply too evil for any kind of relationship that didn't involve them both holding a sword. But even though the sheriff couldn't act in a upright fashion, Robin always did.

In an age of growing egos, fueled by social media outlets and shrinking news cycles, we can learn something important here. Despite the number of views our Instagram or Facebook accounts generate, no matter the number of our Twitter followers, the truth is that none of us are even remotely at the center of the universe. The world doesn't revolve around us. No matter what we have accomplished, we are expendable. When we depart this life, people may say good things about us, and we hope they do, but another generation will arise who never heard of us. The best we can hope for is a fondly remembered picture in someone's photo album, and eventually even that will fade away.

For every famous singer, there are a thousand more who were just as good, if not better, but didn't have a hit song. For every wonderful book ever written, a million more have disappeared, read only by a few fervent fans. You may generate a healthy rant on Facebook that is important and entirely true, but it will not prove as popular as a picture of someone's lunch or freshly baked cookies, to say nothing of a cute kitten.

That's the way the world works. You can either fret and be angry, or you can accept it and do what you can with a smile on your lips, the way Robin Hood approached his life. And if that gets you upset or angry, just remember that of all the real characters in the ballads, the one who is remembered is the one who always seemed to have a good time.

That's a pretty important lesson!

Part IV: The Merry Men

Merry Men: *Ta da, da da da da - whoo!*
Monsieur Hood: *I steal from the rich
and give to the needy...*
Merry Man: *He takes a wee percentage...*
Monsieur Hood: *But I'm not greedy –
I rescue pretty damsels, man I'm good!*
Merry Men: *What a guy, ha ha, Monsieur Hood!*
Monsieur Hood: *Break it down!*
Monsieur Hood: *I like an honest fight
and a saucy little maid...*
Merry Men: *What he's basically saying is he likes to get...*
Monsieur Hood: *Paid!*
Monsieur Hood: *So, when an ogre in the bush grabs a
lady by the tush, that's bad!*
Merry Men: *That's bad, that's bad, that's bad!*
Monsieur Hood: *When a beauty's with a beast
it makes me mad!*
Merry Men: *He's mad, he's really, really mad!*
Monsieur Hood: *Now I'll take my blade and ram it
through your heart. Keep your eyes on me, boys, 'Cause
I'm about to start...!*

(*Merry Men*, from the movie, *Shrek*)

According to the ballads, Robin Hood gathered about him a group who have been remembered as "Merry Men." When I was a child, they were my heroes. All of them. There would have been no Robin Hood without them. Now that I am older, I understand why that was the case. They are as fictional as he is, but that makes them all the more real, somehow. Each of them has a unique personality. Each of them has a specific craft or calling in life. Each of them has a special talent.

These days, I understand that was not by accident. Each was carefully chosen by those who wrote the sagas and sang the ballads, or perhaps invented is a better word, because, like Robin and his antagonists, they each symbolize something.

Nottingham and its common-man reputation has quite a history when it comes to fighting against oppression. Robin Hood and his band may have been the first group to gain such recognition, but the 19th century labor movement, in its fight against the grinding poverty of that day, produced another hero. His name was Ned Ludd, who, like Robin, probably never existed. Like Robin, he was said to have lived in Sherwood Forest. But he rose to fame when he supposedly trashed a mechanical loom which could be operated by the unskilled laborers who were replacing the skilled weavers of the town. His followers, called "Luddites," even composed a song about him, much like the songs that elevated Robin to fame.

Chant no more your old rhymes about bold Robin Hood,
His feats I little admire.
I will sing the achievements of General Ludd,
Now the hero of Nottinghamshire.

Ever since that day, Ned (General) Ludd has been called "The Industrial Robin Hood."

Ludd had his band of Luddites. Robin had his Merry Men. Neither could have acted alone. They needed the support that only a group of highly trained individuals, with unique skills and crafts, could provide. Each contributed to the story.

There is a common theme in movies which involves assembling a team to accomplish a task. The 1954 Akira Kurosawa film, *The Seven Samurai*, and its 1960 remake, *The Magnificent Seven*, starring such luminaries as Yul Brynner, Eli Wallach, Steven McQueen Charles Bronson,

Robert Vaughn and a host of others, do it as well as anyone. But *Oceans 11*, starring George Clooney, Brad Pitt, and Julia Roberts, and *Oceans 8*, with Sandra Bullock, Cate Blanchett, and Ann Hathaway, carry on the tradition in grand fashion.

This literary technique was not invented by those who wrote the Robin Hood sagas. It goes all the way back to the Gospels of the New Testament, where Jesus was said to have carefully hand-selected a crew of twelve disciples to carry out the task of forming the organization that would carry out his work after his death. Five Hundred years before that, the Buddha had done the same thing.

Over and over again, the message is the same: If you have an important job to do, it's best done with a crew. So, who were the Merry Men, what were their unique talents, and why was each chosen?

Alas, the stories vary quite a bit. Sometimes the numbers are augmented, and often even the names seem to overlap a bit. But there are a few well-known stories that have stood the test of time. They always seem to rise to the surface. We're going to examine seven of them. Some of them have been told since the beginning. Others seem to be later additions. But anyone who has ever given Robin Hood even a cursory read or seen some of the movies, will recognize them. They are forever associated with him, and will remain so as long as the old ballads are sung.

Little John: Strength and Allegiance

When Robin Hood was about twenty years old,
He happened to meet Little John,
A jolly brisk blade, right fit for the trade,
for he was a lusty young man.
Though he was called Little, his limbs they were large,
and his stature was seven foot high;
Wherever he came, they quaked at his name,
for soon he would make them to fly.

(From *The English and Scottish Popular Ballads,* Francis James Child, 1888.)

Robin Hood and Maid Marian. Robin Hood and Little John. Those are literary names that go together, just like Sherlock Holmes and Dr. Watson, Sam and Frodo, and even the Lone Ranger and Tonto. They are forever linked in our memories.

The story of how Robin and Little John met has been immortalized. Robin, while out on one of his periodic jaunts, came to a narrow bridge spanning a river. A giant of a man, some versions describe him as being up to seven feet tall, approached from the other side. Each claimed the right to cross first, since the bridge was only wide enough for one man at a time. Robin was armed with his bow. The stranger had only a quarter staff.

Right away we run into trouble. The first mention of a "quarterstaff" in literature of any kind doesn't appear until the middle of the 16th century. That's at least three hundred years after the time when Robin's story is set. The best guess is that it was named "quarter" because it was made from hardwood sawn into quarters, as opposed to a single tree branch. But since some of the ballads simply say "staff," we will have to assume that the big man was carrying a walking staff that was proportionate to his size, and that the word "quarter" was a later addition.

When Robin threatened the man by drawing his bow and arrow, the man appealed, in gruff fashion, to Robin's sense of honor. Robin, never one to back down from a fair fight, retreated to a nearby grove and cut a staff of his own. Then the two had at it.

The stranger eventually overpowered Robin, who wound up soaked in the stream. He was good nurtured about the whole affair, however, and asked if he might be allowed a blast on his horn. When the stranger, in equally good humor, allowed him to do so, a group of Robin's merry men quickly answered the call.

Now outnumbered, the giant was asked his name. When he said he was called John Little, a rather common name in those days, he was greeted with good-natured jokes, over-powered, "baptized" by being thrown into the stream, and christened Little John.

"This infant was call'd John Little," quoth he.
"Which name shall be chang'd anon,
The words we'll transpose, so where-ever he goes,
His name shall be called Little John."

When John asked who it was that he bested on the bridge, and learned that it was none other than the famous outlaw Robin Hood, he revealed, in at least a few of the later stories, that what inspired his mission to Sherwood was to sign up to join the band.

He was immediately welcomed and, with much good-natured humor, as is common among groups of men, be they merry or not, escorted back to the main camp and treated to a feast, with much frivolity and copious amounts of ale. His size, attitude, intelligence, and fighting skill soon allowed him to rise to the top and become Robin's right-hand man.

Besides his strength, Little John is best remembered for his allegiance to Robin. He was utterly and always dependable. When Robin needed him, there he was, ready to do whatever was necessary. In at least one story, after the return of King Richard, and the subsequent restoration of Robin's estate and power, Little John was even appointed the new Sherriff of Nottingham.

The message here seems to be that dependable strength and power is always available to those who need it. Without seeking it out, the worthy will be rewarded by the universe itself with the strength need to carry out the task we are put here on earth to achieve. We don't need to look for it. When needed we will find it in as innocent a fashion as meeting it across a narrow bridge. Then, after receiving it, even if it means a bit of a struggle, we will discover that, all along, it has been seeking us.

Many people refer to this as serendipity. Webster's New International Dictionary defines a serendipitist as "one who finds valuable or agreeable things not sought for." Serendip was a former name of Ceylon, and comes down to us through an old Persian fairy tale called *The Three Princes of Serendip*, the story of three men who had the gift of serendipity, unsought blessings, or gifts of grace.

The Greek word for gifts of grace, *charisma*, has come to be expressed in English as "charisms," or "charismatic." It has both a religious and secular meaning, but for those whose religion is a daily search for meaning in secular life, the definitions tend to blur together. So the word serendipity is very useful—a gift of unexpected grace along the way. It seems to open up the concept of receiving surprise favors from the cosmos.

When Robin saw a giant of a man approaching him, and even challenging him, he never thought he was meeting the man destined to become his second in command. It was serendipity.

I once had the privilege of talking to a very wise ninety-six-year-old woman. She regaled me with story after story of the old days. Since I intended to call next on a very discouraged man in his seventies who never had anything good to say about anything, I asked her what I should say to him.

She thought for a minute and then said, "tell him to remember the good times. There must have been some, and those are the reasons for living."

Serendipity can happen to everyone. The key is to be open and receptive, with an attitude that believes things happen for a reason, and convinced there is some kind of purpose in the cosmos. Whether that purpose comes from "out there," by design, or whether it is invested after the fact, the outcome is the same. An event takes on meaning that both *informs* and *transforms* the future. We become different people because of it.

If we keep this in mind when we apply our metaphorical reading of the Robin Hood story, placing ourselves in the role of Robin Hood, of course, an important insight comes to light. Like Robin, we, too, have "lost" our birthright. We have been denied the rights and privileges afforded us at birth, and been relegated to a position of, supposedly, powerlessness.

Human beings did not originate and evolve to live the life most of us have been forced to live these days. We were never meant, as children, to be forced to sit in straight rows and regurgitate information posing as an education. We were not meant to give up the prime years of our life serving at the beck and call of authorities, symbolized by Prince John and the Sherriff of Nottingham, who dictate our every movement and determine our fate based on *their* wants and needs. We not meant to be confined within a cultural system of "going to work" for a certain number of hours every day. But that is just what has happened.

For thousands upon thousands of years, we measured time by the season. Eventually we moved to measuring it by the phases of the moon. Then those periods were divided into weeks and days. Finally, the days, which only had three times to remember—morning, noon and night—were divided into hours, and then minutes. Now we're into nano-seconds.

Think how pervasive the whole system is. We get used to time before we go to school. TV programs are half an hour, with commercials every few minutes. Then we go to school and have to be there by a set time, or we are punished.

When we go to work, we punch in at a time clock, and work at a job that pays us to produce so many pieces of work at exactly a predicted amount of time. We check out at the same time every day, having worked exactly a predetermined number of hours.

We have times to get up, times to eat, times to watch television, and times to go to bed. And then, when we finally retire from the rat race of time, what do they give us? A watch!

The system is so pervasive that it might seem abnormal to state it so succinctly, but given the number of millennia human beings have been on earth, the whole way of life most of us take for granted is not normal. It is a relatively new phenomenon—an artificial paradigm imposed on us by authorities, such as the metaphorical Prince Johns of the world, who benefit from it. They gain money and power by insuring each and every one of us is shaped, from a very early age, into a specific round peg designed to fit into one of their carefully shaped round holes.

Think about one of the first questions we ask children when they are just starting out the process of maturing into carefully crafted adults? "What do you want to be when you grow up?"

For at least the first 200,000 years of human existence on Planet Earth, that question was never, ever asked. What it really means is this: "What set of skills will you develop in order to ensure that an unseen, often unknown, employer can profit off your life before you get too old to supply his needs anymore?"

The retirement age of 65 was set because folks in control of government and commerce needed to throw a sop to those who contribute to their wealth. They thought folks might be grateful to have a few "golden years" on their own, before dying at the then-predicted age of 70 for men and 76 for women.

Those who object and try to buck this tightly controlled system have been banished to the wilds of a metaphorical Sherwood Forest, outside the parameters of accepted society.

There are still those, however, who, like Robin Hood, try to defy the system. Labor unions, civil rights organizations, entrepreneurship, and worker-support groups, are just a few of the techniques of defiance that have been tried over the years. But, usually, those kinds of movements simply try to reform the system, rather than question the very basis of its existence. An ancient, hunter/gatherer ancestor who lived 12,000 years ago, before the beginning of our current civilization, would never have understood the concept of working for someone else's gain, unless it was done voluntarily.

Never-the-less, that is the system that enslaves us now. Prince John has asserted his power over us. We either play by his rules or get banished to the forest, where life is tough and the skills needed to survive and thrive are, in many cases, long forgotten.

Robin Hood teaches how to live in the forest and defy the system.

- The *first* lesson is that we rarely can do it alone. No matter what our skill level, none of us is strong enough to overcome political, psychological, and physical adversity by ourselves. We need help. If we are true to our values, that help will appear. We might not recognize it as such, but when we need our personal Little John, he will be there.

- The *second* lesson is that when that help appears, it will most likely have been seeking us out all along. We may fight against it, at first. Like Robin, most of us are too self-assured to admit we need help. We may even joust with it a bit. But in the end, the universe will supply our needs.

- *Third*, the help we need will in some way mimic our own talents and abilities, but it will add a new dimension to our current set of skills.

My own experience underlines this. I had dabbled in writing during my career as a minster, a teacher, a musician, and a carpenter. I had written a few books and achieved a modest success. But after my retirement, when my physical abilities had deteriorated a bit and it seemed as if I had finished the work I had come here to do, I met my own Little John, facing me on a narrow bridge. It took a bit of fighting before I came to realize that my career as a communicator wasn't over yet. I had to gather around myself a group of talented people to accomplish what needed to be done, including, first and foremost, a daughter who was willing to take over the technology tasks for which I was not suited, a group of long-distance friends to offer encouragement, and some lost-lost talents which had lain fallow for years. But in the end, I was taught that my life wasn't over yet. In some ways, it was just beginning. I was no longer a preacher and teacher in the sense that I was standing before a congregation or class of students. But the audience, although I can't always see them, is much bigger now, and very much appreciated.

That experience is the subject for a whole different book, but it teaches us that we are all Robin Hood, and we are not alone in our fight against an oppressive system that stands between us and our inherent rights as people who may feel ostracized by forces not of our own making.

It's interesting to note that, in the end, when Robin lies dying, it is only Little John, of all the Merry Men, who is there with him. When the universe sends us strength for our task, it is there until the end.

To this day, if you travel to the village of Hathersage, in Derbyshire, you will find a tombstone marking the place where Little John is supposedly buried. It lies in the churchyard of Saint Michael's, under an old yew tree.

Does it really mark the location of the long-gone body of Little John? Of course not. But in the end, does it matter?

Much, the Miller's Son: Man of the Earth

Robin stood in Barnesdale,
And leaned him to a tree;
And by him stood Little John,
A good yeoman was he.
And also did good Scarlok,
And Much, the miller's son;
There was none inch of his body
But it was worth a groom.

From *A Gest of Robyn Hode* (anonymous)

Along with Little John, the member of Robin Hood's band that is most identified with him, and one who is present in the oldest ballads, is Much, the miller's son. Sometimes he is called Midge, as he appears in the tale of *Robin Hood and the Curtal Friar* and *Robin Hood and Queen Katherine*. Once, he's even called Nick. But it's the same character.

A miller is one who operates a mill, specifically one that grinds flour. It is a humble occupation, but one that is of immense importance. No matter whether you are rich or poor, if you want to eat bread, you need to pay a miller.

That gives us a clue about the symbolism of Much, the miller's son. Sometimes he's pictured as a young and innocent lad of about 12 who, sad to say, is not very bright. His father, in this version, was killed by the invading Normans, and Robin took him under his protection.

Often, at least in the movies, Much kills a deer and is about to be punished by the Normans. The punishments vary. He is either about to have a hand chopped off or his eyes burned out. But Robin turns up to save the day and Much joins the band of Merry Men.

One particularly interesting story tells of Much, or, in this case, Midge, being a simple tradesman on his way through Sherwood to sell his flour. Robin stops him, suspecting he is hiding gold in the sack. Midge opens the sack, but proceeds to throw a handful of flour in Robin's face. Then, with Robin incapacitated, Midge beats the daylights out of him. Robin is so impressed by his cleverness and strength that he offers him a position in the band.

However the story is told, one fact remains. If we ever find ourselves ostracized by the establishment and, like Robin Hood, are defying the odds while fighting back, it's good to remember our roots. We might be talented, and even successful, like Robin, but we all need to retain our connection with the common tasks that human beings have been carrying out for thousands upon thousands of years. Even a successful outlaw needs to eat.

The prayer that Jesus supposedly taught his disciples, "Give us this day our daily bread," applies to everyone, rich or poor. And for that, the humble miller is of paramount importance. If we are going to turn grain into bread, we need the help of a miller. We can't get away from it.

It is all too easy for the wealthy class to forget that they cannot survive without the support of those who supply their daily needs. Bread is a staple of life.

During the French revolution, when Marie Antoinette was told the peasants were starving for lack of bread, she reportedly uttered the famous words, "Let them eat cake." She probably never said it, but she lost her head anyway when the common folk finally said, "Enough!" She learned the hard way that people will only take so much abuse. Even the very rich need millers.

So as Robin fought the good fight against tyranny and injustice, he remembered his roots. We need to heed that lesson.

One person who did just that was the country/pop music sensation, Glen Campbell. Before his hit song, John Hartford's *Gentle on My Mind*, made him a household name, and before he hit the big-time singing hit after hit in the 1960s and '70s while hosting the popular TV show, *The Glen Campbell Goodtime Hour*, he was a musician in Los Angeles, and a key member of the band of studio session specialists who had been dubbed, "The Wrecking Crew."

This was the group who recorded song after song that you will certainly recognize but never knew who you were listening to. When you hear hits recorded by Sonny & Sher, the Monkeys, and the rock and roll groups featuring Phil Spector's legendary "Wall of Sound," as in the immense hit, *You've Lost that Lovin' Feeling*, you are listening to Glen Campbell and the Wrecking Crew. Frank Sinatra's 1966 hit song, *Strangers in the Night*, features Glen Campbell, as does Roger Miller's *Dang Me!*

After Campbell made it big, he had occasion to reunite with his old buddies in The Wrecking Crew. They were initially afraid he might have moved on from them. He was, after all, by a now a big star, with all the hoopla that entails. But when it came time to film a TV special that remembered that outstanding team of unknown and mostly forgotten session players, Campbell insisted on joining them, and endured, with humor and grace, their good-natured jibes about his fame. He didn't forget where he came from. They were there on his way up, contributing, in a very real way, to his success, and he never forgot them.

In the same way, Robin Hood paid attention to Much, the miller's son. Robin is forever paired with the humble man of the earth. Their story is as old as that of Robin and Little John. Together, Much and Little John offered Robin Hood strength and daily bread, the two essentials without which no one can succeed.

Robin knew on which side his bread was buttered, and who buttered it. That's an important lesson for us all to learn and remember.

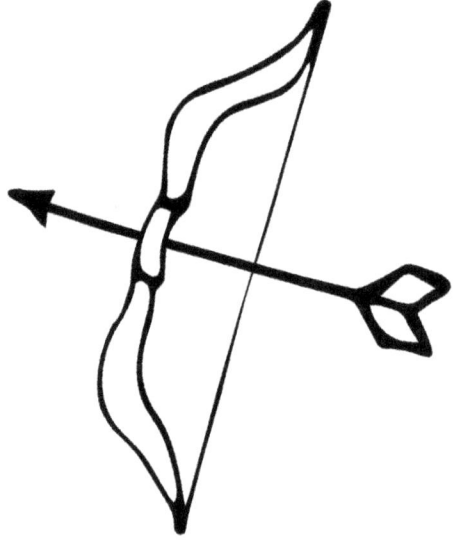

Will Scarlet: Male Beauty and Strength

As Robin Hood walkt the forrest along
It was in the mid of the day
There was he met of a deft young man
As ever walkt on the way.
His doublet it was of silk, he said,
His stockings like scarlet shone,
And he walkt on along the way,
To Robin Hood then unknown.

(*Robin Hood Newly Revived*, from *Child Ballad 128*)

Who is Will Scarlet? The truth is, no one knows. Of all the characters in the ballads, he is perhaps the most enigmatic. We don't even really know what his name is. Sometimes it's Will Scarlet, but he's also variously called Scarlett, Scarlock, Scadlock, Scatheloke, Scathelocke, and Shacklock.

Whatever he is called, however, a Will "Something" seems to be present from the very first tales, right there alongside Little John and Much, the miller's son.

In Shakespeare's Henry IV, Part II, the Bard quotes a ballad about Robin, John, and Will, no last names provided. Presumably "Will" refers to Will Scarlet. But Shakespeare doesn't refer to any character traits, so we don't know for sure.

Never-the-less, he doesn't have a particularly masculine modern reputation, as evidenced by television's *Star Trek: The Next Generation*. In one episode that has garnered quite a lot of fame, Lieutenant Warf, the intensely masculine Klingon, finds himself on the holodeck, dressed as Will Scarlet. He is quite horrified by the part, and considers it beneath his dignity. And in the movie spoof, *Robin Hood: Men in Tights*, Will is portrayed as a swordsman from Georgia, named Will Scarlett O'Hara.

The situation becomes even more confused when Anthony Munday, an Elizabethan playwright, gives us both a Scarlet and Scathlocke, describing them as half-brothers in his play, *The Downfall of Robert, Earl of Huntington*.

To make matters worse, Howard Pyle, in his *Merry Adventures of Robin Hood*, includes both Scarlet and Scathlocke, but includes a third character named Will Stutely.

Whatever his name, he is considered to be the best swordsman in Robin's band of Merry Men. Sometimes he even uses two swords at the same time! Robin is still the best archer, however, and Little John the best with the quarterstaff.

We first hear of Will Scarlet in the group of sagas known as *A Gest of Robyn Hode*, dating back to at least the 16th century. It was recorded on paper for all time some thirty years after the invention of the printing press, so his story was first printed within a few decades of the original edition of the Bible. But here he is first called Will Gamwell.

In this story, he has run away after avenging his father's death at the hands of a steward. He finds Robin Hood and joins his band because Robin was his uncle. Robin, in his own inimitable fashion, renames him Will Scarlet because of the clothes he is wearing.

Although many of Robin's outlaw band are pictured as middle-aged, Will is usually depicted as youthful, the youngest member of the group. But what sets him apart from the others, aside from his skill with a blade, is his love of elegant and flamboyant clothes. Red silk is his costume of choice.

Local tradition says he was killed after a battle with a posse which was sent out by the Sheriff of Nottingham, and is buried at the Church of St. Mary of the Purification, in Blidworth of Nottinghamshire, once a part of Sherwood Forest. A monument to him stands there to this day, but no one knows for sure if he lies under it, or near it, or even if someone by that name ever existed.

With all these variations on the Will Scarlet theme, however, there are two consistencies that provide us with a good handle in determining why the early writers made such a fuss over him. He is always said to be good with a sword, and he is a natty dresser. The sword symbolizes masculinity. The clothes symbolize beauty. The bards believed the two were not necessarily at odds.

King Arthur's Lancelot was portrayed in the same way. There seems to be a tendency in authors from the

Middle Ages to insist that being a "manly" man doesn't mean being a brute. I doubt they would have approved of the men exemplified by wrestling entertainment, as pictured in modern television matches. For that matter, they wouldn't have approved of such shows as *Queer Eye for the Straight Guy,* either. In their view, men didn't have to be fierce to be strong, or gay to appreciate beauty.

Somehow we managed to get away from that in western cultures. But things may be changing. A new term has arrived, and is now being bandied about. It's called "toxic masculinity," and refers to traditional traits, such as physical toughness and aggression, fear of emotions, discrimination against gays, sexual aggression or anti-feminist behavior, that used to be more readily accepted. Even "the strong, silent" types, as portrayed by western movie stars such as John Wayne and Clint Eastwood, are being replaced on the big screen. We have only to see Clint Eastwood's character in *The Bridges of Madison County*, to witness his evolution from Dirty Harry to Robert Kinkaid.

Whereas clothes used to be designed to emphasize success, virility, and power, perhaps best personified by Michael Douglas' performance as Gordon Gekko in the

1987 movie *Wall Street*, and its 2010 sequel, *Wall Street: Money Never Sleeps*, a new generation of men may now be recapturing a bit of what the 13th Century story tellers knew all along. Men can be strong without being overbearing, and independent while still accessible.

This is an important lesson for us today. In fighting for his independence and rightful place in life, Robin Hood could easily have conquered his enemies just as well by using the strength of Little John, while maintaining the earthiness of Much, the miller's son. But if he had done so, he would have been out of balance, a problem encountered by many today who attempt to go it alone.

As I write these words, America is in the process of being torn apart by political forces that represent opposite poles of the spectrum. Both sides feel as though they, like Robin Hood, have been deprived of their rights as citizens.

Those on the political right are usually shown in the media wearing camouflage clothes and carrying military style assault rifles, while sporting large physiques and intimidating attitudes. In churches catering to this kind of man, ministers have been known to urge their parishioners to "keep your bibles open and your guns loaded." The scene has expanded to include women members of congress who insist on carrying loaded guns with them when they go to their Washington DC offices at the Capitol Building, or hunting moose in Alaska with high powered rifles. "Toxic" masculinity is widespread, to say the least.

Meanwhile, those on the political left are often pictured as elite, or effete, intellectuals who shrink from the idea of firearms, and would run from a physical altercation. Whether or not it is true, they are seen as wimps who would rather talk than fight. They are usually dressed in three-piece suits, and would never even think of buying a camouflage outfit. How easy it is for the media to, maybe even unconsciously, portray men such as the openly gay and happily married father of two adopted children, "Mayor" Pete Buttigieg, now the US Secretary of Transportation, as less "manly" than some of his toxic detractors. And Buttigieg is a highly decorated Marine veteran!

Stereotypes die hard, sometimes. The writers who brought us Robin Hood weren't nearly as closed minded when it came to picturing their heroes.

Masculinity refers to the social expectations of being a man. It is therefore derived from particular cultural attitudes. As goes a culture, so goes a man. It is not purely biological in nature. Men are trained from childhood to fulfill certain expectations.

But societies and cultures change over time. Whereas traditionally a man from the Sioux Nation was trained to be a warrior, that was not at all the case in other cultures. Consider, for instance, the changing values associated with American popular culture since World War II.

As the decades of the 1950s began to unfold, a generation of men, who had come home from a popular and victorious war, invented something unique. It was called suburbia. It consisted of white, manicured, neighborhoods that offered a wonderful place for children to grow and thrive.

It was certainly, on the surface at least, an ideal way to grow up. Everything glittered. Beneath the surface, however, pulsed a whole world of racism and inequality that upper-middle-class folks rarely acknowledged. Once in a while it surfaced when the "n" word was uttered or adults spoke about subjects that went way over the heads of impressionable children.

As a product of this gilded age myself, I can still never quite remember what I was thinking about when we were taught how to duck and cover under our desks. On the one hand, I was sure that if the evil empire ever attacked, they would first bomb Grand Rapids, Michigan, where I used to live. But somehow, after the drill was over, I just went home and played Cowboys and Indians, or made what I called "set-ups" with my GI Joe action figures. I simply did not equate war drills with reality. The outside world just didn't exist.

Unless, of course, you considered the music of Elvis Presley. The hair, the shoes, the hips, the guitar, the beat—it was intoxicating. Will Scarlet on steroids!

Speaking for many of my friends, our parents hated it, but what more could we ask! Heroes were no longer those who raised the flag on Iwo Jima. They wore flamboyant clothes and played the guitar.

By this time, we had all become accustomed to TV sets, but suddenly transistor radios were all the rage. No more plugging in! We could take them with us wherever we went. Free at last! Free at last. Thank God Almighty, we were free at least!

In hindsight, the Elvis persona of masculinity had a lot of help. He didn't do it alone. Just when we discovered him, along about 1956, marketing companies discovered us. We had money to spend. It was the beginning of a generations-long love affair between Madison Ave and teenagers. Elvis was soon everywhere, providing the first soundtrack of the Baby Boom generation. The image of "man-as warrior" was changing quickly.

Add all this up while Cadillacs and Chevys got bigger tail fins every year, and what do you get? "The best of times and the worst of times." What it took to be a man had become very confusing. It burst into public view in the 1960s and 70s.

While Elvis was gyrating on stage, Flash Gordon, Davy Crockett, and Zorro were being served up by an older generation who still didn't quite understand that things were in flux. They were the traditional icons of masculinity, but there were hula hoops as well, and various fads such as stilts, roller skates that you tightened to your shoes with a key, shuffle boards and, for some reason, spool knitting.

How did a young boy learn to be a man with this crazy kaleidoscope of images spinning around in his head? Then, as never before, we needed a Will Scarlet. We needed someone who could clash swords with the best of them while dressing like Elvis. *Father Knows Best* and *Leave it to Beaver* gave us men who didn't even remove their suit jackets when they came home from work and read the paper while their dutiful wife prepared a nourishing dinner.

It didn't last. It couldn't. Archie Bunker and "Meathead," his son-in-law, exposed the whole thing and the culture was never the same. Some may say we have not yet straightened the whole thing out.

But until we do, Will Scarlet is a good place to start if we want to discover heroes who teach us how to defy the ego-driven, toxic masculinity that pervades civilizations today, while depriving us all of our inherent right to live a good life, free from the saber-rattling war-mongers and greedy economic enterprises that threaten the very idea of balance and wholeness in today's world, while condemning to a life in Sherwood Forest those who wish to be free.

Alan-A-Dale: The Arts

And when he came bold Robin before,
Robin asked him courteously,
"O hast thou any money to spare
for my merry men and me?"
"I have no money," the young man said,
"But five shillings and a ring;
And that I have kept these seven long years,
to have it at my wedding.
"Yesterday I should have married a maid,
but she is now from me tane,
And chosen to be an old knight's delight,
whereby my poor heart is slain."
"What is thy name?" then said Robin Hood,
"Come tell me, without any fail:"
"By the faith of my body," then said the young man,
"My name it is Allin a Dale."

(From *The English and Scottish Popular Ballads,* Francis James Child, 1888.)

Alan-A-Dale is a late comer to the Robin Hood story. He doesn't show up in the ballads until at least a hundred years after they were first sung, and exactly who he was is a bit of a mystery. He's often confused with Will Scarlet. Sometimes they are both described as musicians.

But history has been kind to him. As more years pile up, his position in the band has narrowed. These days he is not presented as a fighter. He is a minstrel—a troubadour who not only provides entertainment for the band, but, in troubadour fashion, composes the songs that make Robin famous. It is because of his art, the story goes, that Robin became a house-hold name.

It is true that in one account that made its way to television, he is said to be tone deaf. But considering the reputation he has everywhere else, we must remember him as a master musician. Nothing else will do.

Those who fight the good fight against tyranny in government and the work place know how important it is to have a good sound track. It's the artists, poets, and musicians who tell the tale.

Take the riled-up America of the 60s, for instance. It didn't arrive on the scene unannounced. The artists saw it coming. When things started to fall apart, and people started looking for something to believe in, Jackson Pollock and William de Kooning went with the coming times, producing abstract art that ceased even trying to imitate normally perceived reality.

Musicians as far removed as Igor Stravinsky and the Beatles resisted any attempt to be corralled within traditionally accepted forms.

Arthur Miller's *Death of a Salesman* and *A Streetcar Named Desire* didn't even try to make people feel good when they left the theater. Instead, art imitated life. Hollywood epitomized the breakdown of normally accepted behavior. *Bonnie and Clyde, The Graduate, Easy Rider, Midnight Cowboy, The Last Picture Show, The Godfather,* and many more movies that followed, scrapped the idea of "happily ever after."

And you had only to turn on the radio to see that *The Times, they [Were] a Changin'*. The Byrds said it was time to *Turn, Turn, Turn*. As Vietnam raged, Pete Seeger pictured President Lyndon Johnson as being *Waist Deep in the Big Muddy.* Peter, Paul, and Mary were joined by a host of folk groups who dared to question the 60s equivalent of Prince John and the Sherriff of Nottingham.

As always, the artists led the way, even so far as to assure us that *We're on the Eve of Destruction,* at least according to Barry McGuire.

So it is entirely appropriate that Robin Hood had his own musician. It's not by accident that the stories which first told us about him were sung. They were ballads. Even then, traveling minstrels were welcomed with open arms and pocketbooks. They were the ones who knew the landscape.

Alan-A-Dale was just such a troubadour, whether he ever existed or not. If he were not there in the flesh, he *should* have been, and that's enough.

Musicians have changed a lot over the decades. Both Frank Sinatra and The Grateful Dead could fill stadiums in their time. But what a difference in the music! People complained that when the Beatles sang you could never hear them because the girls screamed so loud. They said the same thing about Sinatra. The two acts were separated by a brief time when folk music and jazz went to college. During the 50s and 60s it was "hip" to be quiet and listen to music on college campuses. It came with intellectual appeal and insightful political commentary. That was the kind of scene that probably would have welcomed Alan-A-Dale. One man and a harp, with no back-up band. A strictly acoustic set. Music wasn't just entertainment. It was meant to tell and story and convey the news of the day.

It must have been a popular art form, because so much of it was written down, and later even printed, that we now have a handle on those times. The many quotes we have so far attributed in this book are poems, meant to be sung. Without them there would have been no Robin Hood.

It's interesting to learn how long music has been with us. Probably even before our species. The oldest known instrument in the world is product of a Neanderthal musician who carved it out of the left thighbone of a young cave bear, some 60,000 years ago. It was discovered in a cave near Cerkno, in Slovenia. The artist who made it carved four finger holes for the express purpose of playing some kind of musical scale, and created it at least 20,000 years before any other known musical instrument made by anatomically modern humans.

Even then, folks must have understood the power of music when it comes to affecting emotion. Music's use in medicine has long been recognized as well. Perhaps its first use was as a medicine to relieve pain, spark joy, spread cheer, or sooth troubled senses. We can almost experience the quiet that must have spread through a long-ago forest glade, when the local troubadour tuned up his harp and prepared to sing his latest version of a song meant to transport hearts and minds to worlds far removed from the daily grind of surviving in the wild. That was the task of Alan-A Dale.

It's important to remember this in an age when, more and more in popular forums, music is treated simply as a rhythm to be used for dancing. Dancing is important. Make no mistake about it. But music is much more than that. It is also something way beyond its use as a political weapon, as is so often the case. History is replete with examples of a country using music to emphasize its message or inspire its troops.

When we want to teach stories to children, we often create poems and set them to music. Anyone over the age of fifty or so, and some who are quite a bit younger, can't spell the word "Encyclopedia" without thinking of Walt Disney's Jiminy Cricket. (Just now, when I typed out the word, I found myself doing it in time to the rhythm I learned when I was a child.) And who can ever forget learning the alphabet by memorizing the song that went with it?

Having the metaphorical equivalent of Alan-A Dale in our get-away tool kit is important. After a long day trying to cope with the system of modern civilization, there usually comes a time when we want to identify with the 1970 Clarence Carter hit, "Give me the beat, boys, and free my soul, I wanna get lost in your rock 'n' roll and drift away."

What did Alan's music sound like? We don't know. What kind of a voice did he have? We don't know. What instrument did he use to accompany himself? We assume it was a harp, but we really don't know. Did he sing the words or speak them over plucked chords? We don't know. Out of the one major scale, one pentatonic scale, three minor scales, and seven modal scales we employ today, which, if any, did he use? We don't know.

But the music must have been powerful, to have created and sustained the entire legend, so it behooves us to listen to the soundtrack we are creating of our own lives. It might make all the difference.

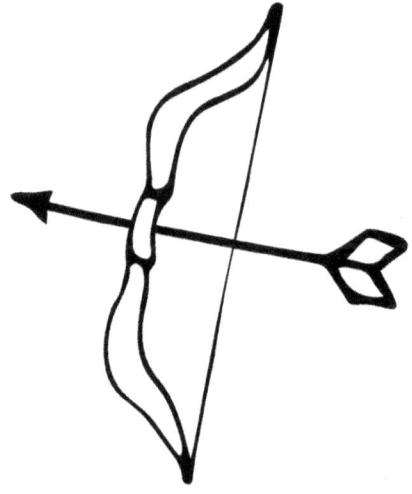

Friar Tuck: Rugged Spirituality

"There lives a curtal frier in Fountains Abby
will beat both him and thee.
That curtal frier in Fountains Abby
well can a strong bow draw;
He will beat you and your yeomen,
set them all on a row."
Robin Hood took a solemn oath, it was by Mary free,
That he would neither eat nor drink
till the frier he did see.

(From *The English and Scottish Popular Ballads,* Francis James Child, 1888.)

From 1972 to 1983, every Monday night it was an American custom to tune in to the television antics of the crew who made up *M*A*S*H 4077,* a medical crew stationed in Korea during the war. A principal character of that unit was Father Francis Mulcahy, played by William Christopher.

His television representation of the clergy was fairly stereotypical. The good father was a bit of a physical wimp, even though he dabbled in boxing and long distance running. But his faith was strong and he was often on the spot when courage or ethical decisions were to be made.

This representation is a pretty standard one when it comes to the clergy. We put our religious leaders on a pedestal, asking them to convene meetings with somewhat uncomfortable prayers, and to be there to say the right things at funerals and weddings. But when real work needs to be done, the tendency is to push them aside until needed again to justify our actions.

During the early 21st century, with roots going back to the late 20th century, this concept began to be questioned by those in the clergy who saw their position as being more prophetical than comforting. Politics, specifically civil rights and the Vietnam war, entered the church in a big way, and spilled out through the media.

When taken out of context, as is often the case when the media wants only soundbites, it can get preachers in trouble. President and Mrs. Obama were forced to quit their Chicago church, the Trinity United Church of Christ, when its pastor, the Rev. Jeremiah Wright, became known for his aggressive public defense of Black Liberation Theology.

The whole idea of docile clergy was foreign to the Robin Hood sagas. Clergy were usually thought to be corrupt. And often, they were. They hid their wealth behind a great deal of superficial piety, but if a good friar expected his clerical garb to protect him within the confines of Sherwood Forest, he was sadly mistaken. Clergy were as susceptible to being robbed as political officials, because they often possessed just as much ill-gotten gains.

Robin was a devout Catholic. In the ballad, *Robin Hood and the Monk*, he risked his life to travel to a Nottingham church in order to pray to the Virgin Mary after he robbed a monk. But he wasn't praying for forgiveness. Instead, he gave thanks, claiming: "Our Lady in the trewest woman that ever yet founde I me!"

During the time covered by the ballads, the people of England were officially Roman Catholic. They readily accepted the Doctrine of the Holy Trinity. But there was money to be had under the guise of collecting for religious purposes, and fat, corrupt monks are commonly found in the literature of those days.

The exception to this rule was Friar Tuck. Yes, he was fat. But he was also a warrior with a jovial, good heart. He and Robin hit it off very well after the customary initiation period.

Robin had warned his men not to accost yeomen, squires, knights, and husbandmen, or farmers. Friars, however, were a different story. In the *Gest of Robin Hode*, he offers these orders:

> *These bishoppes and these archbisoppes,*
> *Ye shall them bete and bynde;*
> *The hye sheriff of Notyinghm,*
> *Hym holde ye in your mynde.*

In the early ballads, Robin is not a revolutionary who sought to overthrow the upper classes. That came later. In these first stories, he is simply seeking justice for honest folk who had been treated poorly by the Norman conquerors.

The first meeting between Tuck and Robin is reminiscent of Robin's first meeting with Little John. It, too, took place at a river. Robin and Tuck approached the shallow ford at the same time. Robin, as was his custom, demanded that the good Friar carry him across. Since Robin was armed, and Tuck wasn't, Robin got his way. But when they reached the other side, Tuck managed to overpower him, and Robin was forced to carry Tuck back across. This continued for a while, with two strong personalities showing their customary good humor while engaging in mock combat.

Eventually, Robin decided to end the whole affair and blew a blast on his horn, summoning his Merry Men. Tuck, not to be outdone, demanded equal time, and whistled mightily, whereupon a pack of huge dogs from the nearby priori showed up to combat Robin's gang.

Robin was so engaged that he asked Tuck to join his band. As was the case with Little John, some of the ballads imply Tuck wanted to do just that in the first place, so they returned to the forest glade for the traditional feast of the king's venison, washed down with copious amounts of ale.

Other ballads tell different stories, usually involving the need for clergy to officiate at a wedding, but this is the one that seems to most often wind up in the movies and on television.

Tuck brings something important to the sagas. I call it rugged spirituality, something the church has often lacked in its two-thousand-year history. It has seen a lot of toxic male spirituality, and more than its share of effeminate spirituality, but very little of the healthy, rugged, male energy that it has so often touted.

To apply this to the modern day, we need to reveal a deeply buried, uneasy truth about Christianity and its formal presentations to the world.

First, I need to emphasize my own credentials before I make the claim I am about to present. I have been a part of the Christian church for 75 years. I didn't just attend, I was part of the inner workings of churches since childhood, in seven states, and served as a pastor in a worldwide Christian denomination for fifty years in a ministry that covered seven churches in three different states. During that time, I participated in ecumenical clergy associations, exposing me to the inner workings of virtually every major religious organization existing today. What I am about to talk about is a well-known fact that is common to them all, and often talked about behind closed doors. But it is not something that people want to readily bring out in the open.

It's similar to a large family gathering where everyone present knows Uncle George is a lush and Aunt Sally has her own set of problems, but no one wants to bring it up in polite company. Here it is, in its perhaps overly-simplified form.

If you attend the monthly board meetings of the vast majority of most Protestant churches, you will find an abundance of men sitting around the ever-present table. They may call themselves deacons, trustees, vestrymen, presbyters, clergy, or something else, but they are predominantly male, and would usually rather be home watching Monday Night Football.

You might readily draw the conclusion that the churches they represent are run by men.

You would be mistaken. Although the common misconception that the church is a male-dominated place reigns supreme, if you camp out in the foyer of a typical protestant church anywhere in the country, you will find a steady stream of women coming and going during the week, and a pretty large majority attending Sunday services and teaching classes in the Sunday School. Women are the ones who really pull the strings, and it's a rather common circumstance throughout Protestantism.

If you move over to the Roman Catholic side of the Christian spectrum, there is an obvious dominance of male clergy, given that women can't serve as priests. But even here, the widespread scandal of homosexual clergy abuse cases that began to break into public consciousness decades ago remains a constant reminder of a less than rugged male spirituality at work.

Move away from religion into the realm more often called spirituality, and the trend continues. Women predominately attend yoga classes and meet in groups that practice meditation and spiritual intention.

We could continue on to explore the cult scene and discover much the same thing. Cult leaders are predominately male, but their followers are mostly female.

Please understand, this is not a bad thing. Church history, from the stories of the Spanish Inquisition and the Conquistadores, to the Puritans of the Salem witch trials, are replete with examples of male toxic energy running amuck under the guise of religion. The feminine presence in religion has, overall, been a good thing.

But, in all things, balance. In the time of the Robin Hood sagas, the masculine clergy were considered to be, for the most part, as corrupt, if not more so, than the political establishment. The troubadours needed an example of healthy, balanced, male spirituality when they composed their Robin Hood ballads. They needed, in other words, a Friar Tuck, who could draw a sword, shoot a longbow, and mix it up with the best of them, while maintaining a healthy relationship with God, even if it meant going against the grain of the established church.

That is the lesson we need to learn from this member of the Merry Men. When we find ourselves at odds with the establishment, through no fault of our own, it doesn't mean we have to give up our spiritual underpinnings. To do so would be disastrous. It would mean turning our backs on a primary source of strength.

But religion, and, for that matter, spirituality outside the traditional borders of established religion, need not be a place of constantly turning the other cheek and giving in to dominating people. As in all things, balance.

Ecclesiastes 3:8, reminds us that there is "a time to love and a time to hate, a time for war and a time for peace." And in the New Testament, the same Jesus who told his disciples in Matthew 26:52 that "he who lives by the sword shall die by the sword," had a different response when told by his followers "Look, Lord, here are two swords." He said, in Luke 22:38, "That is sufficient."

"All things in moderation" means that sometimes we need to emulate the Jesus who made a whip of cords and drove the corrupt money lenders from the temple. Even when we are driven to live in our own metaphorical Sherwood Forest, it's good to keep up a good, rugged spirituality.

There is never a completely male spirituality or a completely female spirituality. Neither shows the way to God, the Source of all Things. To be whole, we need balanced spirituality. It can be a great source of strength

The Saracen: A Mysterious Stranger

ROBIN: *I blame Richard. His task was here at home defending his own people, instead of deserting them to fight in foreign lands.*

KING RICHARD *(disguised as an abbot): What? You condemn Holy Crusade?*

ROBIN: *Aye, I'll condemn anything that leaves the task of holding England for Richard to outlaws like me.*

(*The Adventures of Robin Hood*, Warner Bros. 1938)

During the 20th century, a new character wormed his way into the Robin Hood sagas. While not present in the early versions, storytellers began to mention a mysterious stranger who Robin brought back with him after fighting the Third Crusade along with King Richard. The stranger was a Muslim, and devoted to Robin Hood, presumably because of a debt he felt he owed because Robin saved his life.

In a few late stories, the Muslim, and once in a while his daughter, turn out to be traitors who betray Robin, but these stories don't have a lot of staying power, probably because of the actor Morgan Freeman. In the 1991 movie, *Robin Hood: Prince of Thieves,* starring Kevin Costner, among others, the Moorish-type character named Azeem was played to perfection by Freeman. From henceforth and into the future, Azeem will probably be a permanent addition to the Robin Hood sagas.

Thus it was that a Muslim moved into the prominently Christian neighborhood of Sherwood Forest. But that is a good thing. The late 20th century saw a lot of changes occur in the sagas, due to the evolution of political correctness. Take this exchange between Robin and Guy of Gisborne, for instance, that took place in 2006:

GISBORNE: *There will always be war. So, let's have a king who will fight for our gain—not the pope's.*

ROBIN: *Do you know why I went to war? To recover Jerusalem—to recover our Holy Land. When I got there, I met the Muslims, and the Jews. And I saw it was their Holy Land too.*

GISBORNE: *What are you, Locksley? Lord of the Dance?*

ROBIN: *You're right. There will always be war. As long as people like you revel in their own ignorant bigotry.*

(Episode 8: *The Assassin, Robin Hood*, Tiger Aspect 2006.)

Attitudes about equality and justice evolve, just like everything else. But this is an important point for us to ponder. While fighting a battle against injustice it is too easy to let opinions calcify into a simplistic "us against them." Inclusivity is extremely important. If "my group" does not become "our group," we are headed for trouble.

This important truth was caught in verse by the German clergyman Martin Niemöller in 1946. He wrote a famous poem called *First They Came* ... , in which he beautifully, if poignantly, portrayed the plight of Germans, including himself, who, out of cowardice, allowed the rise of Adolf Hitler, the German equivalent of Prince John, and his attempt to take over the government:

First they came for the socialists,
and I did not speak out—

> Because I was not a socialist.
> Then they came for the trade unionists,
> and I did not speak out—
> Because I was not a trade unionist.
> Then they came for the Jews,
> and I did not speak out—
> Because I was not a Jew.
> Then they came for me—
> and there was no one left to speak for me.

The Holocaust Memorial Day Trust, a charity established by the British government, subsequently published an updated version:

> *First they came for the Communists*
> *And I did not speak out*
> *Because I was not a Communist*
> *Then they came for the Socialists*
> *And I did not speak out*
> *Because I was not a Socialist*
> *Then they came for the trade unionists*
> *And I did not speak out*
> *Because I was not a trade unionist*

Then they came for the Jews
And I did not speak out
Because I was not a Jew
Then they came for me
And there was no one left
To speak out for me

Just because the mysterious Saracen is a new addition to the Robin Hood story doesn't mean it is not an "authentic" part of the tale and thus should be ignored. On the contrary, it means the story is still alive and evolving for new generations. It still holds appeal and is capable of embellishment. It is a living, growing piece of literature that stands on its own. We might even say we live in an exciting time, because the story still can show us new truths and insights during an era totally divorced from its original setting.

Or *is* our era radically different from the time of the first Robin Hood ballads? Throughout this book we have seen that Prince John and the Sheriff of Nottingham live on in the form of political, religious, and economic forces that seek to gain control over us while depriving us of a measure of personal freedom. We know what it is like to be forced to work to provide more money to those who are already rich. We know what it is like to be ruled over by corrupt politicians who want to take away our rights. This isn't new. In one sense, we are all Robin Hood.

The presence of the mysterious Saracen is a reminder that we are not alone in the struggle. Whatever our politics, whatever our religion, whatever our place in life, it is good to recruit others of different persuasions to our cause, because when one suffers, we all suffer. As long as freedom is withheld from one group, or even one person, it is withheld from us all.

That is why America needed to fight a Civil War. That is why nations needed to band together to fight two world-wide conflicts. That is why communities need more than one type of religious establishment to demonstrate different types of traditions. These things do not divide unless we let them divide us. They demonstrate strength, not weakness.

Memories of a so-called Golden Age, when everyone thought the same things and shared the same values, are false memories.

Vestigial Jim Crow laws and white privilege status, corrupt partisan politics, women's rights, the stratification of classes, inequality across the board, and a general attitude of "this is how you do it" authority, proves beyond the shadow of a doubt that memories of a lost era of shared American values overlook great inequalities. The story of Robin Hood, as interpreted in the 21st century, demands there be at least a Muslim or two, or people of color, fighting the good fight along with Robin and his Merry Men. So be it. Swing wide the gates!

With that said, it's time to acknowledge another truth that has remained silent for too long. What about the women? Did Robin lead a band of celibate warriors to victory while awaiting the return of King Richard?

Absolutely not! That's why we saved one of the most important figures in the sagas to the last. It's time to consider the role of Maid Marian.

Maid Marian: Female Energy Enslaved on a Pedestal

A bonny fine maid of a noble degree,
Maid Marian called by name,
Did live in the North, of excellent worth,
for she was a gallant dame.
For favor and face, and beauty most rare,
Queen Hellen she did excel;
For Marian then was praised of all men
that did in the country dwell.
'Twas neither Rosamond nor Jane Shore,
whose beauty was clear and bright,
That could surpass this country lass,
beloved of lord and knight.

(From *The English and Scottish Popular Ballads,* Francis James Child, 1888.)

It would give me great joy to report that somehow those who wrote the Robin Hood ballads understood the role of real feminine strength and importance. I would love to be able to write that they secretly placed symbolism in their stories that prophesied the coming of change, or equality and balance between the sexes—that somehow, they knew something that others of that era didn't know.

Alas, it is simply not the case. The bards of that time and place were just as immersed in cultural male dominance as most of the human race has been for at least the last six or eight thousand years.

"We worship women!" they would say. "We never disparage their role in society! We write only good things about them!"

What they did not understand is that you don't need bars to build a prison. You can lock someone up just as well by enshrining them and placing them on a pedestal, "safe" from the kinds of attitudes that prevail in the rough and tumble world of male ego and self-absorption.

"I'm protecting you honey! Stay at home, safe and sound, while I mix it up out there in the world. Don't trouble yourself with messy things like voting, or politics of any kind. Don't worry about machinations of the workplace. Don't fret about money or making ends meet. I'll take care of all that. You just stay home, take care of the house, and look pretty!"

In 1963, Burt Bacharach and Hal David wrote a song called *Wives and Lovers*, in which they warned women that they needed to dress up when their husbands came home from work, and "run to his arms the moment he comes home to you … I'm warning you!" because "men will always be men," and there are temptations out there in the workplace.

This attitude is prevalent now, and has been for a long, long time. It was no different back in the era of Robin Hood. Women were pictured most often as damsels in distress, capable of swooning, but not much else. When Maid Marian is described, there is always great attention paid to her physical beauty and charm. "She was a gallant dame. For favor and face, and beauty most rare, Queen Hellen she did excel."

In the ballads, and even more so in the movies of the late 20th century, that was her greatest strength. Maybe even her only strength. She existed as a love interest for Robin, because he was a manly man and therefore needed one. The duties of the rest of the women depicted in the stories consisted of cooking, delivering and raising babies, and generally taking care of their men. They might have a sharp, perhaps even respected, tongue, but that was about it. There is no mention of the obvious feminine energy found inherently in nature—energy that, if missing, throws all of creation out of balance.

Modern movies haven't done much better. In 2004, for instance, a movie called simply *King Arthur*, starring Clive Owen as Arthur and Keira Knightly as Guinevere, was touted as being "a demystified take on the tale of King Arthur and the knights of the round table." In the climactic battle scene at the end of the film, Arthur and his knights take on a Saxon army, with Britain hanging in the balance. The men are all suited up for war, dressed to the hilt in armor, carrying swords and shields and appropriate clubs and battle axes. Guinevere, supposedly liberated and a strong feminine presence, while carrying a bow and arrows and ready to take on the hoards right alongside the men, is right in the thick of the fighting. But she has foregone a suit of armor in favor of a bikini. To say she looks a little out of place is an understatement.

There have been times throughout history when strong women leaders stood out. Queen Boudica, who led a revolt against the Romans in 60-61 CE, or Joan of Arc, the "Maid of Orleans," who lived two hundred years after the Robin Hood era, is another.

In modern times, Golda Meir served as the fourth prime minister of Israel from 1969 to 1974. Margaret Thatcher, "The Iron Lady, was the longest-serving British prime minister of the 20th century. Both these women were famous for their strength of character and political acumen. But they are exceptions to the rule. That is simply a historical fact.

So when we read about Maid Marian in the Robin Hood ballads, we have to remember the character of the times, and read between the lines to see what was left out of the story. I'm sure the writers genuinely thought they were honoring her, and thus symbolically women in general. But they had no idea the depths of their society's prejudice, so it never occurred to them that they were simply passing along a deeply ingrained character trait that had existed for thousands of years before them, and still exists hundreds of years later.

The way to learn from this, then, is to read in it an example of how *not* to behave, of how *not* to pass along prejudicial opinions that are entirely without merit, and, indeed, detrimental to society. In other words, we can study the Maid Marian story as an example of how prejudice against women has run rampant throughout our culture.

There is a theory, prominent in some academic circles, that because Marian doesn't appear in the early sagas, but only in later editions, she was invented because by the time people started hearing about her, the upper classes had "promoted" Robin from common robber to yeoman, and then to an Earl. It was their way of sharing in the popular story without suggesting that they had anything in common with a commoner. A "Lord" needs a lady. Hence, Maid Marian.

In 1822, Thomas Love Peacock wrote a short novella named, simply, *Maid Marian*. This was followed by *Robin Hood and Maid Marian*. The two stories present contrasting images of her. On the one hand, she seems to be a rather strong intellectual sort. But she is also portrayed as what can only be described as sexually subordinate to the rest of the characters in the story. Even in the 19th century her identity reveals more about the author than reality.

Mary Wollstonecraft, one of the very first feminists of the 18th century, had written, her ground-breaking treatise, *A Vindication of the Rights of Women: With Strictures on Political and Moral Subjects*, and it had gathered quite a following. Peacock had no doubt been influenced quite heavily by Wollstonecraft's proto-feminist views. In his stories, Marian refuses to be constrained by her father and calcified male domination. She constantly runs off to spend time with Robin in the woods.

Robin teaches her to shoot a bow, and she becomes quite an archer. But she stops short of real membership in the band. Peacock seems to imply that her main function is to insure Robin's reputation. Hanging around with a bunch of men, and men only, might lead to questions about homosexuality. A true hero must forever remain both a fighter and a lover. A gallant lover, to be sure, though an understated one, according to Victorian times.

> *With kisses sweet their red lips meet,*
> *For shee and the earl did agree;*
> *In every place, they kindly embrace,*
> *With love and sweet unity.*

That didn't prevent Marian from fulfilling other expectations, however: "With finger in eye, she often did cry."

She goes on to dress like a page, disguised as a man so as to carry out tasks for the benefit of the band, but she is also not afraid to use her sexuality when it is needed. She becomes, in effect, two separate women, thus embodying the confused roles the feminine mystique occupied in the 19th century. She is powerful and powerless at the same time.

We need to remember these stories were all written by men. This was the same era in which Mary Shelley wrote *Frankenstein*, but she was forced to compose it under an assumed, male name. Likewise, for the Brontë sisters and other now-recognized authors. In their day, women authors were, to put it mildly, discouraged.

What this tells us is that the Maid Marian stories describe feminine attributes as seen through masculine eyes and perceptions.

Now let's apply that insight to the modern day, as we have done with the rest of the figures in the Robin Hood stories. What can it tell us about our fight to defy ego-based forces that cast us away from freedoms that should belong to all, but instead force each of us into our own metaphorical Sherwood Forest?

When the going gets tough, it can be difficult to remember that no matter how strong our feelings and opinions might be, we are all influenced by cultural norms that have been force-fed into our brains since childhood. Just because we might feel strongly about something doesn't mean it's true. We need to work hard at examining our own prejudices.

Did the story of Robin Hood need a healthy dose of balancing feminine energy? Yes! Absolutely!

When it finally came, was it a healthy antidote? Unfortunately, no. The authors probably would not have understood that what they added offered as much harm as good to the sagas. All they did was infuse cultural stereotypes that were part of their social DNA. Maid Marian was invented to enhance the male hero of the story. That's all. Even if she *had* been asked to personify the real female energy found in nature—Mother Earth energy—she probably would have been described as a witch.

What would the stories have become if Maid Marian were described in terms that were more befitting of authentic male/female earth energies? As of yet, we do not know. It has yet to happen.

But, as we have seen, the story of Robin Hood is a changing, growing, and evolving one. It might be that a future author, perhaps a woman, will add the missing pieces that will turn Robin's saga into a balanced, living, breathing representation of healthy human experience. Maid Marian needs some help. One might almost say she needs rescuing. But not by another bunch of male authors. Here's hoping she will soon receive it. Because when she does, Robin Hood will take yet another step forward into maturity.

Conclusions

It's time to draw some conclusions from our analysis of the story of Robin Hood. How can we apply this saga to our present-day plight?

First of all, let's return to where we began this study.

In our time, the metaphorical "Ego of the City" constantly seeks to destroy its wild and untamed predecessor who lives out in the natural world—the world that gave us birth—the world that gave us the freedom which we long ago traded for comfort and predictability.

Robin Hood is a nature man who is at home in the wild forests of Sherwood Forest. He has been forced to return to his roots. There he defies the ego-centric, power-hungry sheriff of Nottingham, who remains ensconced in his fortified urban castle. In the end, Robin teaches us to be victorious by defying Ego's claims on personal freedom and individual choice. He refuses walls and the loss of independence, and fights on until the end, when King Richard, at least in the ballads, returns to put things to right.

The King represents the outside Source of spiritual strength and eventual victory, always waiting in the wings but never arriving to fight our battles for us. Like Tolkien's Frodo, we need to gain our own, personal victory before the return of the king.

Christians await the return of Jesus. Jews pray for the Messiah to come to earth. Indians of the western plains danced the ghost dance to bring back the buffalo and the resurrection of a vanished culture. Eastern Indians prayed for the return of Tecumseh. Many Hindu religions await the final Avatar of Vishnu.

Our source of strength is, indeed, out there, just over the spiritual horizon. But it is also within us. The human condition is one of discovering the inner Source—of fighting for truth and justice. The final chapter is yet to be written. Sometimes it seems to be far, far away, and maybe it is. But none of us can save the world. Saving ourselves is a big enough task for anyone.

Ours is a civilized world, invented and dominated by materialistic ego. Selfish individuality, in the guise of either Prince John or the Sheriff of Nottingham, often appears to be victorious, while archaic Earth Magic seems lost in the metaphorical woods. But in the end, spiritual energies from the natural world, which is a manifestation of the Source of All That Is, offers the hope of triumph over seemingly impossible odds. Robin Hood defies the odds, and is victorious.

He is not alone, however. None of us are. Little John, Much, the miller's son, Will Scarlet, Alan-A-Dale, Friar Tuck, the mysterious Saracen, and even Maid Marian, as flawed a picture as we have of her, each offers a different set of talents and strengths that aid in the battle.

If we look hard, we will find a similar cast of characters surrounding us. There are political, economic, and religious forces at work in the world today that seek to deprive us of true freedom. Unless we play their game, toiling our lives away for their benefit, they cast us out into the wilderness of Sherwood Forest.

In short, none of us are really free. But we don't have to buckle under the tyranny of culture influences, either. If we go about it in the right way, the forest can award us freedom.

We read and re-read the Robin Hood tails because they remind us what it means to live an authentic life in our unique circumstances—in our lives. He is one to whom we can aspire. He is brave and forthright. He triumphs over adversity. He lives his life by his own rules. He gives us hope.

It's not just about the adventure, although that can add spice to the mix. No, the old-timers crafted their tales on many levels. They spoke to a wide audience. One of the deepest and most satisfying levels of wisdom found in Robin Hood involves understanding how to personally respond to an age in which ego reigns supreme. How do we live in a world replete with narcissism?

Earlier we said that when our rulers govern out of a quest for power, when our bosses try to build a reputation that rests on our work and ability, when our friends attempt to use us to accomplish their own ends, Robin Hood shines as an example to follow. Sometimes the only way to achieve real freedom is to fight back, honorably and heroically, even if it means leaving the comfortable world that has been our home and is, indeed, our birthright. At such times, wallowing in self-pity, moaning "woe is me!", telling ourselves that life isn't fair, or that we are being treated with contempt, just won't cut it.

That insight is an important one. How do we apply it?

It might mean leaving the comforts of the city for work in the country. It might involve learning new skills, making new friends, and developing different means of support. But it can be done, honorably and with passionate joy. Robin Hood shows us how. He is more than a historical representation. He is a powerful symbol. He didn't live *back then*. He lives *now*, today, in each and every one of us. He is every man and every woman. As he battles Prince John the usurper and the narcissistic Sherriff of Nottingham, as he faces off against a corrupt church hierarchy who use religion to further their own ends, as he plunders the ill-gotten gains of the ego-encrusted rich in order to distribute them to the deserving poor, he wages a one-man war against the very religious, economic, and political forces that make the world go around today.

We are called to do nothing less. As we said at the beginning of this study, whether or not Robin Hood ever actually ever achieved the adventures credited to him really doesn't matter. What's important is the essence of the story.

But remember that in order to achieve what he did, we have to dare our own metaphorical Sherwood Forest—the place that lies at the center of the two opposite poles symbolized by York and London. There comes a time when we need to learn new skills, new ways of approaching life, new methods of operation, new ways of thinking. The place to learn all that is the place that originally gave us birth. It's a wild place, full of fearsome beasts, untamed people, and mysteries. But it is also a place of wonderful adventure.

There were many who dared to do just that—to join Robin out in the wild, learn from him, and live in freedom. Maybe we, too, need to join his band.

Where is your Sherwood Forest? What do you need to learn in order to live there? How much courage do you have, especially on those long dark nights when you lay awake, contemplating what has become of your life? At such times you need to remember that out there in the wilderness, free from the ego-centered rules of those who would hem you in, there still lies a wild land of mystery. It is different for each of us. But it is there. And it beckons us forward.

Further Reading

Ashton, John and Tom Whyte. *The Quest for Paradise: Visions of Heaven and Eternity in the World's Myths and Religions.* New York, NY: Harper Collins, 2001.

Bolen, Jean Shinoda, MD. *Gods in Every Man.* San Francisco, CA: Harper and Row, 1989.

Bullfinch's Mythology. New York, NY: Gramercy Books, 1979

Campbell, Joseph with Bill Moyers. *The Power of Myth.* New York, NY: Bantam, Doubleday Dell Publishing Group, 1988.

Cotterell, Arthur and Rachel Storm. *The Ultimate Encyclopedia of Mythology.* China: Hermes House, 1999.

Estes, Clarissa Pinkola. *Women Who Run with the Wolves: Myths and Stories of the Wild Woman Archetype.* New York, NY: Ballantine Books, 1992.

Gaskell, G. A. *Dictionary of all Scriptures and Myths.* New York, NY: Gramercy Books, 1981.

Godwin, Parke. *Sherwood: A Novel.* New York, NY: William Morrow & Co., 1991.

Godwin, Parke. *Robin and the King.* New York, NY: Avon Books, 1993.

Houston, Jean. *The Hero and the Goddess.* New York, NY: Ballantine Books, 1992.

James, Simon. *The World of the Celts.* London, England: Thames and Hudson LTD, 1993.

Jones, Prudence and Nigel Pennick. *A History of Pagan Europe.* New York, NY: Routledge, 1995.

Macrone, Michael. *By Jove!: Brush Up Your Mythology.* New York, NY: Harper Collins, 1992

Powell, Barry B. *Classical Myth.* Upper Saddle River, NJ: Prentiss Hall, 2001.

Willis, Jim. *The Religion Book: Places, Prophets, Saints and Seers.* Detroit, MI: Visible Ink Press, 2004.

On line summary -
https://www.boldoutlaw.com/robbeg/merrymen-beginners.html

About the Author

A theologian, historian, and musician, Jim Willis earned his Bachelor's degree from the Eastman School of Music, and his Master's degree from Andover Newton Theological School. He has been an ordained minister for over 40 years.

While serving as an adjunct college professor in the fields of comparative religion and cross-cultural studies, he was the host of his own drive-time radio show and part-time musician. His concern for spiritual growth in modern-day society prompted a series of lectures on historical studies and contemporary spirituality.

Upon retirement, he was determined to confront the essential, mystical Reality that has inspired humankind since the very beginning of time.

A background in theology and education led to his writing more than a dozen books on religion, the apocalypse, cross-cultural spirituality, and arcane or buried cultures, specializing in research bridging lost civilizations, suppressed history, and the study of earth energy, dowsing, and out-of-body experiences.

Other Books by Jim Willis

- Journey Home: The Inner Life of a Long-Distance Bicycle Rider
- The Religion Book: Places, Prophets, Saints, and Seers
- Armageddon Now: The End of the World A to Z
- Faith, Trust, & Belief: A Trilogy of the Spirit
- Snapshots and Visions: A View from the Now
- The Dragon Awakes: Rediscovering Earth Energy in the Age of Science
- Savannah: A Bicycle Journey Through Space and Time
- Lost Civilizations: The Secret Histories and Suppressed Technologies of the Ancients
- Ancient Gods: Lost Histories, Hidden truths, and the Conspiracy of Silence
- Supernatural Gods: Spiritual Mysteries, Psychic Experiences and Scientific Truths
- Hidden History: Ancient Aliens and the Suppressed Origins of Civilization
- The Quantum Akashic Field: A Guide to Out-of-Body Experiences for the Astral Traveler
- Censoring God: The History of the Lost Books
- The Wizard in the Wood: A Tale of Magic, Mystery, and Meaning
- Little Snow White: A Road Map for Our Time
- Merlin the Magician: A Mystery for the Ages

See www.jimwillis.net for reviews and ordering details.

www.ingramcontent.com/pod-product-compliance
Lightning Source LLC
Chambersburg PA
CBHW071442070526
44578CB00001B/188